STUPID FUCKING BIRD

BY AARON POSNER

SORT OF ADAPTED FROM
THE SEAGULL BY ANTON CHEKHOV

★

★

DRAMATISTS
PLAY SERVICE
INC.

2

ACKNOWLEDGMENTS

For Howard Shalwitz... for the opportunity, the insight and the... endlessly intelligent interrogation. Thank you from the bottom of my heart for making this thing happen.

For Maisie Ann Posner... for the inspiration... and All The Feelings.

For Chuck Mee, William Shakespeare, Frank Galati, Brian Mertes, Melissa Keivman, Miriam Weisfeld, Misha Kashman, James Sugg, Craig Wright and, of course, Anton Chekhov... without whom this play would not be whatever the hell it is.

For the many, many actors and other theatre artists—particularly the amazing folks of the original cast and creation team—who helped bring STUPID FUCKING BIRD into being in workshops and readings, and at the Lake George Theater Lab, Woolly Mammoth Theatre, the Theatre @ Boston Court, the Pearl, and so many other places while it continued to grow and change... I have learned from each and every one and I am eternally grateful.

For all the fierce, fervent young artists who seem to be connecting with the passions, fears, frustrations, needs, hopes and longings of the young artists of this play. Chekhov was really on to something! Keep striving. Keep discovering. Make better things! Make things better!

And, of course, for Erin Weaver... for All The Things.

STUPID FUCKING BIRD was originally produced by Woolly Mammoth Theatre Company (Howard Shalwitz, Artistic Director; Meghan Pressman, Managing Director) in Washington, D.C., opening on May 27th, 2013. It was directed by Howard Shalwitz; the scenic design was by Misha Kachman; the costume design was by Laree Lentz; the lighting design was by Colin K. Bills; the sound design and original music were by James Sugg; the dramaturg was Miriam Weisfeld; the production stage manager was Maribeth Chaprnka; the resident assistant stage manager was Jason Caballero; the assistant stage managers were Katie Chance and Becky Reed; the assistant director was Hannah Greene; and the assistant dramaturg was Sam Lahne. The cast was as follows:

CONRAD .... Brad Koed
DEV .... Darius Pierce
MASH .... Kimberly Gilbert
NINA .... Katie DeBuys
EMMA ARKADINA .... Kate Norris
DOYLE TRIGORIN .... Cody Nickell
DR. EUGENE SORN .... Rick Foucheux

STUPID FUCKING BIRD was subsequently co-produced by the Theatre at Boston Court (Michael Seel, Executive Director; Jessica Kubzansky, Co-Artistic Director; Michael Michetti, Co-Artistic Director) and Circle X Theatre Co. (Tim Wright, Artistic Director; Camille Schenkkan, Managing Director) in Pasadena, CA, opening on June 19th, 2014. It was directed by Michael Michetti; the scenic design was by Stephanie Kerley Schwartz; the costume design was by Mallory Kay Nelson; the lighting design was by Elizabeth Harper; the sound design was by Rob Oriol; the video design was by Sean Cawelti; the props design was by Jenny Smith; and the production stage manager was Andrew Lia. The cast was as follows:

CONRAD .... Will Bradley
DEV .... Adam Silver
MASH .... Charlotte Gulezian
NINA .... Zarah Mahler
EMMA ARKADINA .... Amy Pietz
DOYLE TRIGORIN .... Matthew Floyd Miller
DR. EUGENE SORN .... Arye Gross

The New York City premiere of STUPID FUCKING BIRD was produced by the Pearl Theatre Company (Hal Brooks, Artistic Director), opening on March 15th, 2016. It was directed by Davis McCallum; the scenic design was by Sandra Goldmark; the costume design was by Amy Clark; the lighting design was by Mike Inwood; the sound design was by Mikhail Fiksel; the original music was by James Sugg; the production stage manager was Katharine Whitney; and the technical director was Gary Levinson. The cast was as follows:

CONRAD	Christopher Sears
DEV	Joe Paulik
MASH	Joey Parsons
NINA	Marianna McClellan
EMMA ARKADINA	Bianca Amato
DOYLE TRIGORIN	Erik Lochtefeld
DR. EUGENE SORN	Dan Daily

CHARACTERS

CONRAD

DEV

MASH

NINA

EMMA ARKADINA

DOYLE TRIGORIN

DR. EUGENE SORN

THE SYMBOLS IN THE TEXT

/ means that that next line begins here.

— means that the line is interrupted.

… means some new thought, or choice, or change of mental or emotional direction… It also means that the thought continues on beyond the end of the written line. While the actors should pay attention to these shifts, to do so does not require long pauses. The dialogue should be swift and fluid…

* * means that the line between these symbols should be re-written to fit the actual physical attributes of the actor playing the role or the location of the production. It should stay in the tone of what I have written in this version, but should be as detailed (and dicey) as possible in terms of fitting the actual actor. Some variations on "swarthy, talentless fuck-headed pirate" include "smarmy, big-nosed, Ichabod motherfucker" and "smiling, toothy, beady-eyed shithead." Rhythmically, they should all be relatively close to what is now in the script.

THE SET

The first and third acts are designed for some manner of a raw, practical, multi-purpose, transparently theatrical playing space. There is a great deal of flexibility about how it should look, what furniture or props or other things are there, how the play is actually staged, and the use of live music, lighting, sound effects, etc. The action, however, should be relatively fluid and rapid, quite like a

Shakespeare play… The actors who are not in the primary scene are very likely onstage a good deal of the time, around the periphery, playing music, eating, watching, etc. This could vary greatly depending on the space. The second act, however, is imagined to take place in a relatively realistic kitchen with a refrigerator, kitchen sink, etc. Or not. The intention is that it feel somewhat—or even significantly—different than the first and third acts. Or not…

THE ACTING

The acting, of course, should be very, very good: emotionally grounded, deeply passionate, intention-driven, and relatively realistic. Also funny. Pretty much like a really good Chekhov play. Only different, too… In this odd little world, moreso than in Chekhov, everyone is actively grappling for the best way to express themselves nearly all the time, to give words to their frustrations, hopes, passions, and desires. Therefore words often come tumbling out before the thoughts are entirely formed. Everyone thinks relatively quickly. Contemplative is not our friend. The way the actors engage with the text and with each other should be fierce and visceral. Also… love is important. Very important. Love is all over this play. Genuine, deep, real, complex love. If you are ever at sea around choices… tip towards more love and you won't be far off.

THE THEATRICS & META-THEATRICS

The characters are "real" people living the story of the play. They are also characters in a play. Both things are true at the same time. They should all be fully invested in the reality of their lives in the play and the stakes are high and entirely serious. At the same time they always know that they are in a play, that there is an audience out there, etc. etc. There is no "real life" equivalent to this theatrical reality, no matter how much some actors might want there to be one. This is a play. There is simply more than one reality going on at a time. That means the actors can "watch" or be present for other scenes they are not in and they don't have to have the information contained in that scene. They are all part of a play. But there is no separate "actor" character.

STUPID FUCKING BIRD

ACT ONE

0. Start

Con comes onstage, perhaps alone, perhaps with the whole ensemble. He looks hard at us—his intrepid audience—and then talks directly to us...

CON. The play will begin when someone says: "Start the fucking play."
(When someone does, the actors take their places, music starts, lights shift...)
By the lake. In the fall. Late afternoon...

1. Disappointing

Dev and Mash—pronounced "Mosh," like the pit, not like what you do to potatoes—are mid-conversation. They are close, complex, long-time friends. There is a kind of love there, and some odd but powerful kind of connection and familiarity... just not the kind of love either of them wants from the other...

DEV. Seriously. Why?
MASH. Why do I...? *(She touches her black clothes somehow...)*
DEV. Yes. Why?
MASH. What do you think?

DEV. I, ummm…

MASH. *(Absolutely dry/ironic.)* Black is slimming.

DEV. *(Beat. Realizes she is joking…)* Seriously.

MASH. *(Can you be honest, ironic, angry, and funny, all at the same time…?)* I'm in *mourning*. For my *life*. I'm un*happy*.

DEV. Wow. Okay…

Are you *that* unhappy?

MASH. You're an idiot.

DEV. Yeah, maybe. But…

MASH. What?

DEV. Nothing.

MASH. What??

DEV. Nothing.

But… my life is worse than yours. I mean… *so* much worse… And you don't see me wearing black. *(He is dressed partially in black.)* I mean, sometimes, but it's not, like, a *thing*… But, Jesus, my life is way worse than yours, you know?

MASH. How is that even possible?

DEV. I'm poor.

MASH. *I'm* poor.

DEV. I'm way *poorer*. And lonely and, you know… *sad* most of the time. And I tutor kids for tests I utterly don't believe in, which is just an insane way / to spend—

MASH. Well, I'm a cook. Part-time! That's not even a real job…

DEV. I have flat feet… which hurt, you know… all the time. Plus I'm an orphan, so that's… you know… *unsettling*.

MASH. *(Almost tossed off…)* What are we, in a fucking Dickens novel?

DEV. And I'm unhappy in love! *I'm unhappy in love…* I mean, you know I love you ridiculously and you, you know, barely tolerate me… But mostly I'm really, really *poor*. *And *lonely* and *chubby* and *bald*.* And I'm sorry, but that's actually much harder than mourning your lost… lonely… broken… *whatever*.

MASH. Ah.

DEV. But I'm still… *whatever*. *Hopeful.* I still have hope. You know?

MASH. Wow, "hope." *(Pause…)* You can be happy if you're poor.

DEV. Yeah?

MASH. Yes.

DEV. Oh. Well…

(He genuinely considers this. Then, having reached a conclusion:)
No.
So when is Conrad's... *thing* starting?
MASH. Soon.
DEV. And what is it, exactly?
MASH. It's a "Site-Specific Performance Event."
DEV. What's a...?
MASH. It's kind of like a play but not so stupid.
DEV. Stupid?
MASH. No one's pretending to be someone else.
DEV. Oh. *(Quick beat, working that out...)* Then what do they do?
MASH. They... *behave.* They say things and do things, or whatever, but they're not pretending to be, you know, *Bob* and *Trudie.*
Like fucking five-year-olds playing house. It goes deeper than that.
It's *art...*
DEV. And Nina is in it right?
MASH. *(Dark and small.)* Yeah...
DEV. That's nice. That Con and Nina can connect that way. *(She sees where he is going with this from before the word go...)* That she can be part of his... *creation...* part of his *work,* you know? That they have that in common. That they can *connect* on a whole other level, while we—
MASH. Please shut the fuck up, okay? For a minute. Could you do that?
DEV. Okay.
MASH. Please?
DEV. Okay.
MASH. Please?
DEV. I said okay.
MASH. Thank you. *(Beat. Big picture.)* I'm sorry. I just... *can't.*
This... *(She gestures to him and her together, somehow...)* I just *can't.*
Okay?
DEV. I know. *(Beat.)* It sucks.
MASH. Sorry.
DEV. Yeah. Okay. *(Dev starts to leave...)* See you at the... *thing.*
MASH. *(Sits... Then turns to us.)* I wrote this. It sucks, but...
Don't judge.
> YOU'RE BORN AND THEN YOU LIVE AND THEN
>   YOU DIE
> YOU NEVER GET TO KNOW THE REASON WHY

YOU BREATHE AND THEN YOU DON'T, YOU'VE
   JUST BEGUN
YOU'RE HOT YOU ROT, AND THEN YOU'RE DONE,
SO WHERE'S THE PART OF THIS THAT'S FUN?

LIFE IS A MUDDLE, LIFE IS A CHORE
LIFE IS A BURDEN, LIFE IS A BORE
THIS APPLE IS ROTTEN RIGHT DOWN TO ITS CORE
LIFE... IS DISAPPOINTING
YOU LOVE AND THEN YOU LOSE THAT MUCH IS
   SURE
THAT'S JUST THE WAY IT IS, YOU MUST CONCUR
YOU HOPE AND LIKE A DOPE YOU'RE WRONG
   AGAIN
YOU TRY YOU DIE SO WHY BEGIN
IT'S ALL A GAME YOU'LL NEVER WIN...

LIFE IS A MUDDLE, LIFE IS A CHORE
LIFE IS A BURDEN, LIFE IS A BORE
THIS APPLE IS ROTTEN RIGHT DOWN TO ITS CORE
LIFE... IS DISAPPOINTING
(To the silent audience.) Shut up.
*(Mash leaves. Some kind of shift, maybe. Or not. A moment later Con
enters, excited, hurried, nervous, energized. He sets up what he needs
for his play...)*
SORN. *(To us...)* By the lake. Near an ancient little outdoor stage.
Approaching dusk...

2. The Stark-Naked Heart

*Nina arrives breathlessly, excited, exuberant, flustered, nervous...
This whole scene has a slightly frantic, positively charged, geared-
up energy to it...*

NINA. Hi hi hi...
CON. Where the hell have you been?

NINA. I'm so sorry—

CON. How can you *always* be / late? You're like a genius of lateness, a fucking—

NINA. *(All run together.)* I know, I know, / I'm sorry, I love you, I just couldn't—

CON. Well— *(Hearing "I love you.")* —okay, good, all right.

NINA. Can I just—? *(Meaning can she change her clothes right there...)*

CON. Sure.

NINA. *(She starts changing clothes, making-up, etc. She might well be briefly naked or naked-ish or semi-naked, enough to have a visible effect on Conrad...)* I'm so nervous!

CON. You're gonna be great!

NINA. *(During all of this she continues to prepare.)* I remember your mom performing down here when we were little. She was always so unbelievably good...

CON. Yeah...

NINA. Won't she kind of hate it that I'm performing here now...?

CON. *(Terse.)* She'll love it.

NINA. And are they really coming? Both of them?

CON. I think so. She said so. Though you never know / with my mother...

NINA. What's he like?

CON. Who, Trigorin?

NINA. Of course.

CON. Jesus, I don't know...

NINA. Oh, c'mon. You've met a bazillion *(Note: that means "very many"...)* famous people with your mom, but I never get to meet anyone, so / I'm *curious.*

CON. He's fine. He's *quiet* and *humble* and and and *unassuming* in this very assuming little way that makes sure you can't help but notice how humble he is.

NINA. I love his work.

CON. You do? I didn't know you'd / read anything—

NINA. Not that much, really, just *The Laughing Dog Laughed* and his first book of short stories, *The Stark-Naked Heart.* But they're / *amazing.*

CON. I've never read any. Are you almost ready? Do you / need to...?

NINA. Really?

CON. What?

NINA. You've never read *anything*?

CON. No. Why?

NINA. Even since your mother and he have / been—?

CON. Especially since then. I mean—you know?

NINA. No. Sometimes I don't think I understand you at all.

CON. *Excellent.* And on that note—

NINA. Or your play, for that matter.

CON. Perfect.

NINA. What if they won't talk when they're supposed to?

CON. They will.

NINA. But what if they won't?

CON. Then they won't.

NINA. What if they hate it?

CON. Then I'll shoot myself in the head. *(Now reassuring her.)* They won't hate it.

NINA. What if they hate me?

CON. You're perfect in it. Radiant. Ideal.
They'll all fall completely in love with you. Trust me.

NINA. I do.

CON. Good.

NINA. Oh, look!

CON. What?

NINA. *(Struck. Excited. Not too precious...)* Holy cow-sie-dotes! Look at that seagull. So... *elegant.* And I've never seen one so amazingly *white* like that. She's almost glowing from the sunset...

CON. *(Trying to go along with her...)* Yeah... it's really pretty.

NINA. Just look at her, Connie...! *(He does for a moment...)* She's just... floating up there above it all. Not a care in the world. That breaks my heart a little, somehow. *(Playful.)* And it looks like we're wearing the same dress! *(Nina might even, if so inclined, fly around the stage a moment or two, playfully...)*

CON. Are you, umm, ready?

NINA. I think so.

CON. Excellent. Have fun.

NINA. I will.

CON. You're awesome.

NINA. And you're a genius.

CON. And you're my only muse!

NINA. *(Lovingly admonishing...)* Enjoy this!

CON. *You* enjoy it!
NINA. No *you*! *(He grabs her and kisses her. Not long, but very nice…)*

3. I Like Art

*Folks enter for the "showing": Emma, Con's mother; Trigorin,
her lover and a famous author; Sorn, Emma's older brother;
Dev, Con's best friend; and Mash, his mom's cook/helper. They
find places while Con and Nina finish preparations… Emma
dominates the scene as she does pretty much any scene or room
she is in. She is always performing herself to some extent…*

SORN. No, I do, I do, I *like* art. I find it… *comforting.*

EMMA.	DEV.	TRIGORIN.
Oh, Jesus…!	Me, too. I like art…	Ummm… well…

TRIGORIN. … you might want to refrain from sharing that with
certain people…
SORN. Who?
TRIGORIN. Artists, mostly.
SORN. Artists don't like art?
TRIGORIN. Well, no, / actually…
EMMA. … but that's a whole other thing. My point is most of them
don't particularly strive to make art that's "comforting," big brother.
SORN. Oh really?
EMMA. The poorer, the more tortured the artist, the better the
art. I believe that's the conventional wisdom.
DEV. *(A throw-away…)* Then I should be a genius…
EMMA. Van Gogh and his like really fucked the goose on this one.
SORN. You don't think it works that way?
EMMA. I think it is self-flagellating horseshit.
TRIGORIN. *(Amazed, amused…)* Okay then…!
EMMA. Certainly some great artists have suffered, of course they
have, but I'm sorry, I don't think abject misery or a… weepy soul is
the best measure of quality, no.
DEV. Then what is?
EMMA. *(An absolute, and, she knows, controversial conviction:)* Success.

DEV. Oh. Well... TRIGORIN. Fascinating. SORN. Truly?
EMMA. It may sound crass, but it's true. If people *want* to see
something—want to pay their hard-earned money to see it—that
means something. Something *tangible.*
MASH. But you're not saying unpopular art is bad art, right?
EMMA. No. Maybe not. But I'm sure as fuck not saying it's better
art, either.
DEV. Self-flatulating? What does that even mean?
SORN. *Flag*ellating.
DEV. Oh...
CON. *(Appearing from behind the stage...)* What isn't better art?
SORN. The man of the hour!
EMMA. And speaking of tortured artists... our playwright!
MASH. Do you need any help?
How about Nina? Does she need   CON. *(To Mash.)* No, thanks,
anything?   I'm fine.
CON. *(Quickly.)* I think she's fine, thanks. *(To everyone.)* Okay, is
everyone here?
SORN. I think so.   EMMA. Of course.
TRIGORIN. *(To Con.)* Well, thanks for letting me join you...
CON. Sure. Although you've made my leading lady kind of nervous,
she—
EMMA. Who, him? Nonsense, he's a pushover for a pretty girl. *(In
the lightest, most joking and delightful way...)* It's me she should be
worried about!
CON. Perfect.
MASH. You sure you don't need—
CON. *(Snippy. She has asked before...)* I'm fine!
DEV. Excellent. I was just saying to myself today, I could use a
good "site-specific performance event" to spice up the fall.
CON. Shut up!
DEV. Do we have to... wear masks or something?
CON. Okay, soooo... Thank you all for coming. The name of this
piece is... *HERE. WE. ARE.* It's a work in progress, and this is our
first showing, so we / are really just...
EMMA. We understand, darling. It's just a rehearsal...
CON. No, not a rehearsal, a *showing.* It's / not that we haven't...
EMMA. Okay. "A Showing," / sorry...
CON. Anyway. Right. Right... Okay, here we go.

4. Here We Are

The play begins. It should be good. Or as good as it can be. It should certainly be taken absolutely seriously and they should be trying their best. It is earnest, evocative, passionate, and a genuine attempt to affect those in the audience. The part we see is an invocation as much as anything, an attempt to actually shift the perceptions and focus and energy of the audience in a real way. Con perhaps controls the lights, plays music, runs things off a computer or something to make it all happen. There are all kinds of ways to go about this, but it should not be stupid or overly pretentious or silly in any way. When Nina appears she looks wonderful and surprising. There should be some beauty...

NINA. Here we are. Here We Are.
Here. We. Are.
This is real, this is true,
This is new, this is now...
A new place.
A liminal space,
A place of grace
And the boundless pursuit
Of beauty
A place where truth
Might be told—
Where streets
Are not lined with gold,
But just maybe with something better—
Unfettered
Possibility,
Lively Maybes
And vital Why-The-Fuck-Nots
Not people like robots,
All piping the same tune,
The tried and un-true

The Nothing-Ever-Really-New...
Not a fictional tract
But a *fact*.
Not just *art*,
But a *start*.
(Music abruptly ends, just as Emma is caught saying...)
EMMA. *(Under her breath.)* Oh, Lord...
MASH. Shhhhhh!
NINA. *(Suddenly eye-to-eye with her audience...)* So. Here We Are. Aren't we? Aren't we here? *(Turning abruptly to Sorn, who is caught off-guard.)* You, sir. Are you here? *(Beat.)* Are you here?
SORN. Umm...
NINA. Are you here? A simple question. Are you here with me, with *we*, now?
SORN. Umm... I think so...
NINA. Good.
(Turning to Emma.) And you, ma'am. Are you here?
EMMA. It certainly seems that way...
NINA. Oh.   TRIGORIN. *(Gently.)* Emma...
EMMA. *(To Trigorin, and the assemblage.)* She asked the question...!
NINA. But... but if we're all really here, then where are we really? What is this place, this sacred space where we've gathered for this one moment in time?
EMMA. My back yard.
SORN. Shhhh!   TRIGORIN. Shhhh...   EMMA. Well, are we
                                     supposed to answer or
                                     aren't we? I'm just—
(Lights and music shift. Nina lands this at least partially on Emma...)
NINA. Here we are.
Here We Are...
Not in a lie
Not some
Time-Gone-By Fable
Or Far-Fetched Fairy Tale
Nothing stale
Not a retread or a rehash
Nothing tarnished or trashed
By hacks or the hackneyed,
By starlets or star-turns
By has-beens who've crashed and burned...

18

This is just This.
This is just This.
This is just This.
This is just This.
This is just what it IS,
Not some bullshit show-biz,
Not a reference to another place
Or another time,
Not some Once Upon A Kingdom built on Rhyme
And meter, but something sweeter,
A place and a moment
So patently *un*-true
It just *might* be new.
So different in feel
It might be realer than real.
(Music out. Lights shift...)
So where are we now? Are you still in the same place you were five
minutes ago? What is going on inside of you right now...?
EMMA. I don't think she really wants to know...
TRIGORIN. Shhhh...   SORN. Please...
EMMA. Oh, come on, is this a joke? Connie, is this really your *play?*

CON.	SORN.	TRIGORIN.	DEV.
Mother, for	Let her finish...!	Emma!	I think this is
Christ's sake...!			it...

EMMA. What? What? She's tromping around in my back yard on
my fucking stage /
TRIGORIN. Calm down now, sport...
EMMA. wearing my dress and telling me... what...? That the plays
I do are—
CON. It's not about you!
EMMA. Oh really?!?
CON. All right. That's it. We're done here. Nina, get off the stage!
*(She does, awkwardly, and with all possible alacrity, looking at the
dress she had no idea was one of Emma's old ones...)*
EMMA. Oooooh, is this a part of it, too?

TRIGORIN.	SORN. *(To Emma.)*
Emma, please...!	Pumpkin, you really shouldn't...

CON. If you can't even—I mean, if you can't even—Fuck it!!!
(As he storms away, wounded and hurting...)
Fuck it fuck it fuck it fuck it fuck it!!!!!

5. Worked Up

EMMA. Now what the hell?
MASH. I'll go find him, okay?
EMMA. What was that all about?
TRIGORIN. You offended him.
EMMA. He offended me!
SORN. He was trying to impress / you.
MASH. Should I? *(Go and find him, she means…)*
EMMA. With *that*? / Seriously?
DEV. I thought it was kind of great.
EMMA. Oh, for fuck's / sake…
DEV. I was really feeling *here*.
MASH. Ummm…
EMMA. Yes, yes, go, go, tell him I want to talk to him, would you?
MASH. Of course… *(She leaves quickly…)*
DEV. She was really good…
TRIGORIN. *(With an inadvertent, telling tone…)* Yes, very charming.
EMMA. Oh, come on, that… *pretentious drivel* was an attack on me! He's trying to show me what he thinks of the plays I do by forcing us to— He said it was a play, and—
DEV. A "performance event."
EMMA. What?
DEV. You said "play," but I think…
SORN. Where is she?
TRIGORIN. Why are you so upset?
SORN. Is she still here? Nina?! Nina?!
NINA. *(Coming out.)* Hello?
SORN. Brava! Well done! *(There is polite applause from everyone…)*
EMMA. Lovely, my dear, well done. *(She walks away from the group a bit…)*
NINA. Thank you so much.
TRIGORIN. Indeed. Lovely… *(Introducing himself.)* I'm Doyle Trigorin.
NINA. Oh, I know. I've read your books. Well, not all of them, but—you know. A lot.
TRIGORIN. Thanks. I'm glad…

DEV. *(Pushing in…)* Nina, that was great!

SORN. You were ravishing, my dear. I'm only sorry it was so brief.

NINA. Oh, there was a lot more.

SORN. Oh, that's too / bad…

TRIGORIN. Well, maybe some other time.

NINA. I should go and see if I can find Connie…

EMMA. *(Thinking of Con…)* Oh, dear…

SORN. What is it?

EMMA. I guess I've really upset him. He's *so* sensitive. The *smallest thing*—

SORN. Yes, well, he is a human being.

EMMA. What is that supposed to mean?

SORN. We're *all* sensitive. Much more than we let on, I think.

TRIGORIN. I think that's very true.

SORN. Thank you.

DEV. Absolutely. Very… you know… *true. (Beat.)*

TRIGORIN. I find it amazing, this… human capacity to *care.* *(Even though this is not about her, per se, he's never unaware of Nina during this.)* And I hate to say it, but I've noticed it makes shockingly little difference what one chooses to care about. I see people get so unbelievably… *worked up* over remarkably mundane things. A shade of paint. An unkind review. Whether the muffins will make it to the big meeting in time… even though no one ever seems to eat the muffins at the meetings, as far as I can tell. But still: muffins there must be! Or heads will roll!

NINA. You don't get… worked up?

TRIGORIN. I prefer the 100 Years Test.

SORN. What's…?

TRIGORIN. Will anyone care in 100 years? About the muffins. Or the color of your kitchen cabinets. Or the relative success of your… latest novel or your… back yard meta-theatrical skit. If—

SORN. Fascinating test…   DEV. I love muffins.

TRIGORIN. I'm sorry?

DEV. Oh, nothing. I just—I love muffins. A really *good* muffin. I just really like them.

TRIGORIN. Ah…

NINA. Well, I should probably really get going…

TRIGORIN. *(Impulsively trying to keep her there…)* Must you?

EMMA. *(Ending the conversation.)* Well, don't let us keep you. Well done.

DEV. Great job, Nina, that was… *(He makes an explosion sound and gesture…!)*

TRIGORIN. Wonderful work, truly…

NINA. Thank you, that means the world to me…

EMMA. We need to get you into a real play some day. You know, with a plot, and characters, and words that mean things when you say them.

TRIGORIN. Emma…

NINA. That's all I want. To be an actress. Like you.

EMMA. Then I am sure that's what you'll do. Goodbye, then.

NINA. Goodbye. Oh, and so sorry about the dress, I had no idea…

EMMA. You keep it. You look wonderful in it. Doesn't she?

TRIGORIN. Certainly. Like a young *Rita Hayworth*.

EMMA. *(Tossed off, to Doyle.)* She doesn't know who that is…

NINA. *(To Doyle.)* So nice meeting you. *(To the rest.)* Goodbye everyone!

TRIGORIN.	SORN.	DEV.
Take good care…	Great work!	Nice job, Nina.

EMMA. *(Leaving. Snarky…)* Well, what a delightful "performance event." If only she'd been juggling, naked, and covered in chocolate! *(She turns back and sees Trigorin is not following her.)* Are you coming?

TRIGORIN. Of course.

EMMA. Are you all right?

TRIGORIN. Absolutely. Are you?

EMMA. *(Heading off…)* Couldn't be better. Children and art! What fun…!

SORN. I'll be along presently.

EMMA. *(Almost off…)* Suit yourself.

DEV. *(To Sorn, once they are gone…)* Well, I liked it.

SORN. Yes. Me, too. Very much.

DEV. "Here We Are."

SORN. Indeed…

DEV. Anyway… I'm gonna go see if Mash found Conrad. Or if I can find him. Or her. Or… Whatever. G'night.

SORN. Good night.

6. So Much Feeling…

SORN. *(To us.)* Well… I thought it had something. The "play." Or whatever it was.
I mean… where are we, most of the time? You know? *Where are we?* You ever have that feeling where you were just somewhere and then suddenly you're some other place and you think… how the hell did I get here? And that's bad enough when you're just, you know, driving to the store or something… but when it's sometimes years at a time… or a decade. Like, what the hell happened to my forties? I mean, I know I was there, I can show you my tax returns… But where the hell was I? Was I really living my life? Day in, day out. *Where was I?*
(Launching into a story to illustrate his point…) When I was maybe six or seven I had a turtle named Mr. Hardtacks. And one day there was this—
MASH. *(She is deeply upset and shaken under her calm exterior…)* Did he come back?
SORN. I'm sorry?
MASH. Conrad. Did he come back?
SORN. No.
MASH. I couldn't find him.
SORN. He'll be along when he's ready, I'd imagine.
MASH. Yes. Right. *(She starts cleaning up, putting things away…)*
SORN. Are you all right?
MASH. *(Tight, not okay…)* I'm fine.
SORN. All right. *(Quick beat.)* You sure?
MASH. I'm fine.
SORN. All right. *(He looks at her for another moment…)* Would you like a Life Saver?
MASH. What?
SORN. A Life Saver. *(Reading.)* Tropical Fruits. *(Taking out the Life Saver, looking at it.)* I think it might be coconut. Or guava. Not mango. Something white. *(Holding it out to her.)* Would you like one?
MASH. Would I like *a Life Saver?*
SORN. Yes.

MASH. *(Bursting into tears.)* I love him so much. I love him so much and he is never ever going to love me back. I hate my life. I hate it I hate it I hate it I hate it I hate it...

SORN. *(Goes to her and puts out his arms, still holding the Life Saver, and she comes into them like a little girl. He hugs her...)* Shhh... there, there. There there.

It'll be all right and all... Shhhhh... *(The Life Saver in his hand is getting awkward... While still hugging her he pops it in his own mouth... Beat...)* So much *feeling*.

TRIGORIN. *(From elsewhere...)* Later that same night. Down by the lake...

7. New Forms!

Con talks to Sorn and Dev. Late. Con is restless, pacing, frustrated, confused... He holds a copy of his play, which he is tearing into pieces...

CON. She loves me not *(Rip.)*, she loves me *(Rip.)*, she loves me not *(Rip.)*, she loves me *(Rip.)*, she loves me not *(Rip.)*, she loves me *(Rip.)*, she loves me not *(Rip.)*, she loves me *(Rip.)*, she loves me *NOT!*

SORN. Oh, please... You *know* she loves you.

CON. I don't know...

SORN. You can see it.

(Con makes a guttural grunt of denial...or something...)

DEV. *I* can see it.

CON. I can't. Not anymore...

SORN. She loves you...

CON. She sure has a weird fucking way of showing it.

DEV. But that doesn't mean she doesn't love you.

CON. I don't know...

SORN. But she's your *mother*.

CON. So? You really think every mother loves her son? You don't think that deep down a lot of them kind of... you know... *hate them*?

SORN. Oh Connie...

CON. All the *sacrifices*. All the *energy*. The *money* and *time* and *poop* and *mess* and *stress* / and *stretch marks* and *wrinkles*...

SORN. I don't know. I'm not exactly an expert on family matters...

CON. Oh, come on, you know your little sister as well as anybody. You've had to deal with her since she was *born*! You know I'm right. She doesn't for one second want to think about the fact she has a grown kid. Dye and Botox can't make me go away. The math of me. I mean she had me at nineteen, not nine. So if I'm *this* old, then she has to be *that* old, and she just kinda hates me for that...

SORN. I can see how you might think that...

CON. And she knows I fucking hate the "art" she makes. Those awful, stupid movies and those ridiculous plays she does. *Mrs. Winthrop's Cat* or *Turn on a Sixpence* or whatever the fuck...

DEV. That last one got great reviews...

CON. Oh, please!

DEV. You don't like plays, now? I thought you loved the theatre / more than—

CON. We need new kinds of theatre! *New forms!* I mean, fuck, do you have any idea what's passing itself off as theatre these days? Do you ever go?

SORN. Umm...

CON. No, no I know, you think you "should," but do you ever, of your own free will?

DEV. Do you know how much / tickets cost—

CON. I mean, this theatre, this one, where we're doing this show right now, this one is better than most, maybe (who knows anymore), but Christ what they're doing to Shakespeare these days to make him "*accessible*"... and the tiny, tepid, clever-y clever-y clever-y little plays that are being produced by terrified theatres just trying to keep ancient Jews and gay men and retired academics and a few random others who did plays in high school trickling in their doors...

Do you know that six people is now a big play? Seven or eight, like this one— *(Instantly out to the audience.)* (Yes, of course I know I'm in a play, I'm right here and you're right there, and since you can see and hear me let's just assume I can see and hear you, too, and when you pick up your playbill, like you did earlier, sir, to see... I don't know... *whether I've ever done a show at Arena Stage or if Rick's ever been on Broadway* or where to eat after the show, I saw you.

25

We all see damn near everything you ever do out there, all of you, just so you—I'm not blaming, we're glad you're here, we're totally grateful, actually—but just so... you know, you know...). Yeah, a play like this one with seven actors is practically un-producible. If we weren't a... whatever... a a a deconstruction... a rip-off of a classic— *(Looking at a picture of Chekov on the set if there is one. If not, cut this line.)* *Thank you! And fuck you!*—we probably wouldn't be here right now, you know? You know?

SORN. Ummm...

CON. But seriously, Good Christ, we need new *forms*, new *passion*, new *ideas*—something *real*, you know? Something *REAL*. Or what the fuck's the point?

DEV. Like this?

CON. What?

DEV. This play we're in right now. Is this the kind of new work you mean? New forms?

CON. No no no. *Fuck* no! Better than *THIS*! Amazing! Brilliant! New forms of theatre that can actually make you feel like living *better* or *fuller* or or or... *MORE*.

DEV. But what / kind of...?

CON. We need new forms that are actually, actually, actually NEW! New forms that open up new possibilities, new ways of being in the world. We need bigger hearts! We need wider minds and better ideas and we need them *now. (Yelling.) We need them NOW!* I mean, don't you feel that? Don't you? *(Turning to audience.)* Don't *you*? *(Very quick beat.)* Don't answer that. That's rhetorical!

SORN. How about—

CON. Don't you dare say fucking Cirque du Soleil fucking *Fuerza Bruta* whatever the fuck to me, big-ass spectacle, because that is not what I am talking about, I am not talking about eye-candy and diversion.

SORN. No, no, I was—

CON. Sorry. Sorry, what were you going to say?

SORN. *(Trying to come up with a lie...)* I was... I... No, you're right I was going to say Cirque du Soleil. *(Con laughs, not ungenerously, but still ironically...)* No, I just saw them once, and I thought it was kind of...

CON. What?!?

SORN. Wonderful. I thought it was kind of *wonderful*.

CON. Yeah, me, too.

SORN. Oh. But then—

CON. But nothing *changed*. Nothing in *me*. Nothing in the *world*. *NOTHING!*

It's like the hand-job of the theatre. Sure, nice, fine, there's some pleasure involved, sure, but nothing real has actually happened, nothing worthwhile has been exchanged or has transpired. Nothing real. Nothing *real*. You know?

SORN. But why do you—

CON. What?

SORN. Why does it need to change things? Why do you want to change things?

CON. Are you kidding me? Are you kidding me? *Why do I want to change the world?* Is that what you are actually asking me?

SORN. Yes. I mean… yes.

CON. Have you seen the world lately? I mean actually, actually *seen* it?

DEV. *(Under his breath.)* Here he goes…

CON. *Rampant stupidity. Inconceivable greed. Legitimized fear-mongering and xenophobia and the global glorification of mean-ness and indifference to suffering…* Selfishness and neediness achieving new heights never before even imagined. Old forms. Old forms of everything, always being *called* New, but never actually *being* new. And new technologies and media onslaughts and and and, fuck, whatever… *BREAKFAST CEREALS* appealing with assassin-like accuracy to every worst impulse human beings have been subterraneanly cultivating for the past ten thousand years. Why do I want to change the world?

BECAUSE IT NEEDS CHANGING!

And once upon a time, somewhere, maybe in Eastern Europe—at least in the Eastern Europe of my imagination—"The Theatre" was something that could maybe be some tiny, tiny, tiny part of that… and it has got to find its way to be that again or it should go the way of the dodo and the bell bottom and the newspaper and just GO AWAY!

SORN. Wow.

CON. Yeah. Wow.

(He abruptly walks away, or storms out, or… Emma enters… or maybe she has been there all the time, watching along with other cast members…)

DEV. Emma's turn. To have her say…

8. Perfect Parenting...

EMMA. When he was little I used to make my hand die.
He'd be... screaming or whatever... and if he wouldn't stop, I'd tell
him he was hurting me. I'd tell him... I'd tell him he was killing me,
actually, that's what I said, I said, "You don't want to kill Mommy,
do you?" And then I'd... make my hand die. Like this... *(She makes
one hand slowly, sadly, wither and die... Not a joke. A sad, pathetic,
emotionally manipulative symbolic death designed to make a little kid
obey without question...)* And he'd get this little look on his face...
and he'd stop. It was very *effective*.
I can't help but think now that that was not, perhaps, perfect parenting.
But it worked... And I needed things—*anything*—that worked...
I was eighteen when I got married. Eighteen fucking years old.
Hardly out of diapers. To my first famous leading man. Dixon.
Dixon McCready, remember him? No, me neither... Jesus, the way
he said his own name should have tipped me off... "Dixon. Dixon
McCready. Rhymes with seedy." Oy...
"Sexual harassment that just worked out" we called it. I thought
that was so funny and charming at the time. Like we'd beat the
system. What did all those "adults" who thought they knew better,
that told us to wait, that told me I was too young, what did they
know? I *knew*. It was true love! It was perfect.
"What could possibly go wrong?" I asked my mother during one of
our stupid, endless fights. "What could possibly go wrong?" Well,
as it turned out... *things. Many things* could go wrong... And did.
Wonderfully, impossibly wrong, and at twenty-two I had my first
hit movie, my first tabloid scandal, and I was a divorced mother of
a two-year-old son. And the universe said... "Well, good luck with
that..."
So, yes, that's right, my point is, indeed, don't judge. Don't you
dare judge me.
You've done it all perfectly, have you? Love. Life. Career. Family.
Fidelity. Passion. Well, all right then. Now, those of you who are...
socially responsible, deeply fulfilled, vegan, charitable, millionaires...
who work out and have sex three times a week, *you* can judge. But
the rest of you... *shut up.*

I'm doing the best I can.
I don't hate him. How could I? I don't hate him.
But he does... *bother me.*
(Music. There is a movement interlude. The stage gets rearranged. Time passes. This represents the flirting, frustrations, missed connections, broken hearts, unspoken longing etc. etc. of the two days that pass. We see all kinds of dynamics. Nina and Trigorin flirt, in some way. Con is hurt and upset. Emma is... bothered. Dev is focused on Mash, Mash is focused on Con, Con is focused on Nina, Nina is focused on Trigorin... you get the idea...)
MASH. *(To us.)* Two nights later. Drinking. And eating pie.
Pie that *I* fucking made...

9. Actually, Actually...

Con is now starting to lose it a little... things are getting pretty bad and he is moving rapidly towards the edge, towards desperate... Perhaps Doyle and Nina at least remain onstage in some way so Con can reference them...

CON. She's killing me!
DEV. You need to calm—
CON. She's literally driving me insane!
DEV. Literally?
CON. All right, *figuratively.* (Tiny beat.) No, *literally.*
DEV. Listen, Nina adores you. She's just—
CON. We were doing fine. I mean... fine-ish. And then along comes that... *swarthy, talentless fuck-headed pirate*... and suddenly it's like I'm—I can't catch my breath, like I'm drowning or something, like I'm, like I'm...
DEV. In space?
CON. No, like I'm... like I'm fucking drowning! I need a beer. Want one?
DEV. No, I'm fine. *(Con walks off. Dev turns to us...)* Yeah, so, this isn't good. Trigorin's a great writer and all, but he's... *kind of an asshole.* I mean, he's Emma's *guest.* And *lover.* And the way he's flirting

29

with Nina is just not right. It's almost as bad as the way she's flirting with him… Not that anyone seems to notice, except Con… who's freaking out like someone just fucked his cat. And me. That's the advantage of everyone thinking you're kind of a boob… they don't tend to think I notice things, but I do. Everything, pretty much. (Which is why I love Mash so much. Isn't she amazing? Underneath…?) *(Con has reentered and interrupts him…)*

CON. How can I win her back? How can I get her to love me the way I need her to?

DEV. Oh, biscuits…

CON. How can I get her to love me the way I love her?

DEV. You are SO asking the wrong person.

CON. It must be possible.

DEV. Bullshit.

CON. It must be!

DEV. Why?

CON. Because Nina is my life. *My whole life.* I've loved her since since since… Look, I know what love *is* because of her. And now I'm screwed, because love has… *attached* itself to her. And while this might be the hokiest thing ever said anywhere by anyone, ever… she IS love to me.

DEV. *(Laughing a bit, despite himself, at his friend…)* Yeah, well, that is a little—

CON. Fuck you. You just don't understand how *unfair* love can be, or you / wouldn't—

DEV. *I* don't understand? I don't…—??? Listen, the woman I love— the woman I'm, you know, *burning for* every day—is ridiculously, stupidly in love with *you*. And has been for *years*! Years!!! Now what exactly is it that I don't understand?

CON. *(Micro-beat.)* That's not true.

DEV. Of course it is. We all know it. We all know it. We pretend we don't, but we do.

CON. Ummm…

DEV. So, waddaya say?!? You think I can get her to fall in love with me instead? You think love is logical? That is makes sense? That it obeys some *laws*??? My love for Mash hurts me. Do you understand that? I *long* for her.
I feel it in my *thighs.*
Who ever heard of a love so powerful your *thighs* ache???

CON. Your *thighs*?

DEV. Yes. My *thighs*. It's ridiculous...
(Beat. There is just nothing—or too much—to say about this. So going on...)
CON. I wish I didn't know Nina so well. Then I could lie to myself better. But I know every look, every pause, every... cloud of an idea that crosses her face.
You should see her looking at him. And then looking at me to make sure I didn't see her looking at him that way. Then looking away from me after she knows I've seen her looking at him, and then trying to look at me kinda the same way she was looking at him so I won't feel SO BAD, and then FAILING epically at at at at *replicating* the look when I am the focus... I mean not even *close*.
I can't fucking believe this is *actually, actually* happening.
DEV. Maybe it's actually, actually *not*.
CON. But it is. It IS! I can't sleep, I can't eat (except pie, somehow pie is exempt...) but I can't fucking *function*. How is that good? How is love fun? How can I— *(Turning to the audience.)* How can I get her to love me again? You've seen her, you've seen us, how can I get her to love ME more? *(Beat.)* I'm really asking. *(Beat.)* I'm actually, actually asking. Does anyone have any ideas...???
DEV. They're not going to talk.
CON. They might.
DEV. They know you're fictional.
CON. So what? Half the things about most of the people they know are at least twice as fictional as I am, and the other half are only about half as interesting. But I bet that doesn't stop them from giving *them* advice. *(To the audience.)* Seriously, how can I get her to truly see me for who I am and to love me *fully* and *entirely* for that? Anyone??? Seriously. I'm actually, actually asking for your help...
(He engages the audience in a discussion about what he might do to get Nina to love him. He tries to actually, actually get them to talk. He listens to their ideas intently, asks further questions when appropriate, tries to get them to give him helpful, practical advice. Hopefully someone says something about a gift, or about letting her know who you are, or to show her, or do something, or says something that helps to move him towards a new idea. An idea that requires immediate action. An action he sets out at that moment to undertake...)
Right. Right. Good. Thank you. That's very helpful. Thanks.
(He leaves...)

DEV. The next day. Down by the lake. Con sent Nina a note. *(Dev somehow has a copy of it. He reads it to us.)* "Meet me. Noon 30. The Place. Con."

10. Hope Dance

Nina is waiting by the lake. It's just about 12:30. She waits. There could be a song or some music here. Then, almost by default, she talks to us...

NINA. So, there's this story of his called "The Tiny Sacred"—it's in his first collection, from when he was even younger than Conrad is now, I think—and there's this little orphan girl in it. Her name is Annabelle, but they call her The Thimble.
Isn't that great?
And she has... consumption, or something, so she lives mostly in her tiny little room, mostly in bed, and she creates these imaginary worlds within worlds in the swirls on her bedspread and things like that...
But when things are particularly bleak... she does the Hope Dance. On her bed. All alone. At night. The Hope Dance. Don't you love that?
So when I was maybe, oh, twelve or thirteen or so, after one particularly terrible day—you know, evil step-father, drunken rage, poor me, blah blah blah—one night I just got up on my bed in the middle of the night and... I did it. I did the Hope Dance. And I instantly felt better. *He* gave that to me. He gave me that *gift*.
And now he's right here. And... and he seems *to like me*. Me! While he was talking to me last night and I got weak in the knees. That's a thing that actually happened. My knees got *weak*... he touched my arm right here for, like, two seconds, and I swear it *burnt me*. I mean... What am I supposed to do with that?
(She hears something that might well be a gunshot... off someplace... it startles her, changes the course of her thinking, not necessarily knowing why...)
I love Conrad, I do, he's great... And he loves me so much it seems...

(Maybe confessing quietly something she has never said out loud before.) Well… it seems kind of *rude*… or *awkward* not to love him back.

And I do think he's totally amazing and really talented, but…but…

(Mash appears…)

11. Can I Help You?

MASH. Oh.

NINA. Oh, hi. Were you—

MASH. What?

NINA. Looking for Connie?

MASH. Why?

NINA. You weren't?

MASH. No, I—whatever.

NINA. You were?

MASH. Yes. What about it?

NINA. Nothing, I just… I haven't seen him. He should be here soon, though. He asked me to meet him here.

MASH. Of course. Okay… *(She goes to leave…)*

NINA. Mash?

MASH. How can I help you?

NINA. How can you—? Umm…

MASH. Don't stress it. I was being *ironical.*

NINA. I know. I'm not stupid.

MASH. I never said you were.

NINA. I didn't say you / did.

MASH. I know you're not stupid.

NINA. And I know you're not.

MASH. Okay. We're neither of us stupid. So… how can I help you?

NINA. I just wanted… I just wanted to say… I'm *sorry.*

MASH. For?

NINA. You know… "All The Things."

MASH. You're sorry?

NINA. Yes.

MASH. For "All The Things"?

NINA. I am. *(Beat.)*

MASH. *(Accepting it as her due.)* Good. See you later. *(She starts to leave...)*

NINA. Good luck.

MASH. Fuck you.

NINA. Okay. Mash?

MASH. Yes???

NINA. Can I just say... fuck you and your little black cloud! I didn't do anything to you ever. Not ever! You can star in your own little lovelorn tragedy until the end of time and wear, you know, sackcloth and ashes on your soul, but / the universe

MASH. What the hell does...?

NINA. is not out to get you and no one here has DONE anything to you (especially me), and I think you know that, and if I were you I would / get my head

MASH. I can't believe...

NINA. out of my ass and take a good look around and / and and...

MASH. Jesus...

NINA. you know... *make some fresh choices*!!!

MASH. Gosh, thanks for the *relationship advice*! You're really the person I look to—

NINA. *(Strong. Clear. True.)* Just because I'm me doesn't mean I'm wrong. And just because you're meaner than me doesn't mean you're right.

MASH. Wow.

NINA. I'm just sayin'...

MASH. I— You have no— Okay. Okay...

(She walks away. But she walks away thrown and genuinely rattled... and actually, actually considering what Nina has just had the balls to say to her...)

12. Stupid Fucking Bird

Con enters abruptly, carrying a bloody bird-filled sack. He is taut, tense, edgy. He just shot a fucking seagull to demonstrate his love. He is not at all well... He lays the bloody bag down at Nina's feet, ceremoniously, creepily, hopefully... He hopes she might be able to see this symbolic act exactly as he intends it— as a desperately serious esoteric demonstration of his undying love for her... It all, of course, starts to go desperately wrong almost immediately...

NINA. What's that?
CON. A bird.
NINA. A bird?
CON. I shot it.
NINA. Shot it? You shot it? You shot a *bird*?
CON. Yep.
NINA. Why? *Why?*
CON. Hard to say.
NINA. What kind of bird?
CON. I don't know.
NINA. Is it a seagull?
CON. Why?
NINA. I don't know.
CON. Yeah, it's a seagull.
NINA. Really?
CON. *(He knows...)* I don't know.
NINA. What kind of bird is it, then?
CON. Some Stupid Fucking Bird, how should I know, just some Stupid Fucking Bird!!!
NINA. Did you really shoot a bird? Is there really a dead bird in that bag?
CON. Yes.
NINA. Is it a seagull?
CON. Yes!
NINA. And you shot it???

CON. Yes!!! It was fun. I'll be next.

NINA. What?

CON. *(Wildly.)* Chances are!!!

NINA. What does that *mean*?

CON. I'm losing it! I'M LOSING IT!

NINA. Connie, what's happening / to you? *(Perhaps at this moment there is a shift in reality. Lights. Sound. Either abruptly or perhaps slowly creeping in bit by bit… The following questions start out rapidly, but almost kind of normally and pretty much reasonably, but soon spin out of control and grow in extremity…)*

CON. What happened?

Where did you go?

Why did you leave me?

Are you mad at me?

What did I do to you?

Did I do anything to you?

Are you mad at me?

Do you hate me?

Do you think less of me than you used to? Do you think I'm a bad person? Am I ugly or not sexy in quite the right way? Am I a bad kisser? Is there something about me that you can't quite name but just don't like?

Do you hate my jokes? Do I have bad breath? Am I not funny enough? Do you want someone who is better at things? Someone taller? Someone thinner? Someone richer? Smarter? Happier? Funnier? More talented???

Are you mad at me?

Do you just kind of hate the way I am around you when you don't know a word or haven't read a book I've read or something and so I'm kind of careful and kind and kind of jokey but also condescending and you can tell that I kind of hate that you haven't read that book or know that word?

Are you upset or pissed or angry or hurt that whenever we fight or disagree or either of us gets tense or upset or frustrated or annoyed about any little thing, any nothing little thing, I somehow find some way to make everything all about ME in all kinds of small and subtle ways that leave you no room to be mad at me but no real space or agency of your own?

Is that why you're mad at me?

Is that why you don't look at me like you used to, with your whole self?

Are you yearning for something you sense you're never going to find with me and are therefore looking for in the most unlikely but obvious place, that being of course the bed or affections of my mother's boyfriend the famous fucking rich fucking charming fucking fucking fucking fucking *author* whose very presence on the earth diminishes me and makes me feel like one of those broken little limp dead mice that Atticus The Catticus used to bring into the house and drop in front of you when we were young and small and happy and free???

NINA. Connie, I—

CON. Oh, look. Here comes Trigorin.

NINA. *(Instantly looks around to see him...)* Where?

CON. Oh. Okay, Great, excellent, gotta go, take it slow, see ya later. *(He leaves.)*

NINA. Wait, what are— Con. Con!

(She watches him go, wants to say something more, but there is nothing to say, so... she just... doesn't. Then Trigorin appears...)

13. Oh, Nina...

TRIGORIN. Hello, Nina.

NINA. Hello, Mr. Trigorin.

TRIGORIN. Please, Doyle.

NINA. Excuse me?

TRIGORIN. Doyle. It's my name. Please / call me Doyle.

NINA. Oh, I know I know that.

TRIGORIN. I thought I'd just come and say goodbye. I saw you down here.

NINA. Oh...

TRIGORIN. Well, I should go pack. We're leaving today. Suddenly. A whim, it seems.

NINA. Oh. *(Beat.)* I'm sorry.

TRIGORIN. For what?

NINA. That you're going.

TRIGORIN. So am I. *(Quick beat. Maybe he turns to go...)*

NINA. May I... ummm...

TRIGORIN. Yes?

NINA. Ask you a question. May I ask you a question?

TRIGORIN. Of course.

NINA. Well. I've just been wondering... I just really want to know—oh, it's stupid.

TRIGORIN. No, go on.

NINA. What does it feel like? To be *famous*. What does that *feel like*?

TRIGORIN. Ah...

NINA. And a genius, too! What does it feel like to be a famous genius?

TRIGORIN. *(He smiles. Just smiles...)* Oh, Nina...

NINA. Why are you laughing at me?

TRIGORIN. I'm not. It's just that... it's... It's not something you *feel*...

NINA. That can't be true. You *matter*. People write about you and think about what you say. *You have the ear and eye of the world.* That must feel like *something*.

TRIGORIN. I know why you think that, but it's not true. Not really. Suppose a thousand people are thinking about something I wrote right now. Or a hundred thousand. Or even a million. Well, wonderful. But, also... *so what?* I can't feel that. I can't hear what they say... or feel their adoration. Fame isn't actually really anything...

NINA. But to *write* great works of literature. To write *Hamlet*!

TRIGORIN. But I didn't write *Hamlet*.

NINA. I know that.

TRIGORIN. *(A toss-away...)* I wish I wrote *Hamlet*...

NINA. You wrote "The Tiny Sacred." You wrote "The Unguilded Lily" and "The Queerest Girl in the World." You wrote "The Silent Song of the One Good Shoe." Those stories are amazing. They changed my life.

TRIGORIN. I'm glad. I really am. And yes, the act of creating can be wonderful. But that is different than fame. A wonderful phrase will occur to you, suddenly, fully formed, and you realize, you *hope*, that maybe no one else has ever put that idea together in *quite* that way before. That can be very nice...

Or you capture something... rare... *and shining...* just right.

But genius—if I have any at all—never feels like genius in the moment. *On the day.* More like...obsession. Compulsion. The unassuageable itch that rules your life... The need to create, to call

38

something new into being is absurd. *Arrogant.* Insane, really... I mean... *why?* Aren't there enough *things* already? Do we really need more? And yet on we go. More books. More plays. More painful poetry poured out in the small hours by proverbial candlelight. And the songs!!! My God, the songs alone...! Sometimes I think there should be a moratorium on the creation of Art for 100 years. Let's just take a good look at everything we already have and then maybe decide what else we might need.

NINA. But isn't it wonderful to know you matter? I think living in the hot spotlight of the world's attention—would be *wonderful.*

TRIGORIN. Oh dear...

NINA. But why am I wrong? What do you mean you can't feel it?

TRIGORIN. All right... what does it feel like to be beautiful?

NINA. Oh, I'm not—

TRIGORIN. Let's not lie. All right? We're having a serious talk. Let's not lie.

NINA. Okay.

TRIGORIN. You Are Beautiful. Period. So... what does it feel like? What does it feel like to radiate loveliness like... *sunlight?* What does it feel like to have perfect breasts? *(She turns sharply away. He gets flustered...)* I'm sorry, I'm just— I I I was trying to make a point. I didn't mean to say that. I I I was just—

NINA. *(Turning back.)* Then you *don't* think they're perfect?

TRIGORIN. *(Beat. Taking in her surprising cheekiness...)* No, no, they are. it's just— Well, it's like that, then. It's like that. You can't spend all day just thinking about what perfect breasts you have, can you? I mean, *I* might be able to, but *you* can't. They're just a fact of you. Literally a part of you. Well, fame is like that. But not as good. Fame isn't even real. It's not something you can hold in your hand.

NINA. Unlike my breasts.

TRIGORIN. I'm sorry?

NINA. *(Quite surprisingly boldly. Though perhaps timidly/boldly... she has never done anything like this before. And never expected she would...)* You heard me.

TRIGORIN. Yes. Yes, I did...

NINA. Don't you want to?

TRIGORIN. Hold... um...

NINA. Yes.

TRIGORIN. *(Answering her.)* Yes.

NINA. Why don't you then?

TRIGORIN. Right. Well. Right... *(She approaches him. Quite close...)* Here you are.
NINA. Here I am.
TRIGORIN. Yes.
NINA. Here. We. Are.
(Beat. Lights. Music. Everyone enters...)

14. Want

NINA. I just want to be loved.
CON. I just want to be loved.
DEV. I just want to be loved.
SORN. I just want to *love*.
MASH. I just want to *be* loved.
EMMA. I just want to be loved *madly, dangerously, FULLY...*
TRIGORIN. I want something... *superlative*. Something *fresh*. Something...
SORN. I just want a hug, really. A hug that lasts *a month*.
MASH. I just want to hurt less...
CON. I just want to be loved *more*.
DEV. I just want to be *In Life*. You know? Right in the middle of it. Not on the outskirts, the suburbs, the periphery of my *own damn life...*
NINA. I just want to shine! I want to ignite the world for one, hot, shining moment like a flame or a shooting star or a *meteor*! I just want to be a *meteor*!
EMMA. I'd really just rather not be hated anymore. I've been hated for one thing and another since I was a little girl and I would just like... a fucking break from that.
DEV. I want a bottomless bowl of ice cream. A bowl the size of a *bushel basket*. And I want it to be brimming full of wonderful ice cream and it's all mine... but I can share it if I choose. And I have a little pouch with a variety of... *esoterically twisted long-handled metal spoons*... and I can let whoever I want use one of these marvelous spoons, and the ice cream is like... pear cardamom or cranberry and clove, or whatever weird-ass flavor I want it to be.
SORN. I just want us all to be kinder. Or at least try to be.

TRIGORIN. I want sweet first kisses. Inconceivable softness. *Discovery…*

CON. I just want things to be like I always imagined they could be.

MASH. I just want him to *look at me.*

SORN. I want to be twenty-seven again. I think I'm ready to do my late twenties really well now…

MASH. I want him to look at me and see me so he has some fucking clue about who I "actually, actually, actually, actually" *am!*

TRIGORIN. I want a lot, really. As much as possible of what life has to offer. I mean, I'm sorry, but I do. Not Either/Or. *Yes/And.* I want as much of everything wonderful I can possibly get because this is life, this is all there is, so why the hell not?

EMMA. I just want to be the center of attention. I mean, fuck it, if we're being honest, that's what I want. All eyes riveted on me because I am a sacred vessel for art and I've worked my ass off and I fucking deserve it. I want Adoration and Respect from Everyone, Always and Forever.

NINA. I just want love to be everything and fame to be what I've imagined and to be bathed in rose petals, cool rain, and endless applause. I want that!

CON. I just want it ALL TO FUCKING STOP!!!

(Con abruptly runs offstage or out of sight. A beat or two. Loud gunshot. The others start! Blackout. Music…)

End of Act One

ACT TWO

A kitchen. Perhaps this is a lovely, rustic, fully functioning, realistic kitchen with a kitchen sink, food, drink, etc. Perhaps merely the suggestion of all that… But it needs some kitchen things. Music. Lights up on Trigorin and Mash. She plays her ukulele and sings. Trigorin sits watching her and drinking slowly and deliberately… They have been drinking for a while. It is late evening, the day after the day on which Con shot himself in the head… and mostly missed…

15. What Could Be Harder…?

MASH.
  I WANDER THROUGH LIFE IN A HAZE
  EACH DAY AN UNMAPABLE MAZE
  MY HEART HAS BEEN BROKEN, MY HEART HAS
    BEEN BURST
  THE BEST THAT LIFE CAN OFFER ME IS MORE OF
    THE WORST…
(To him.) Don't judge.
  NO TWO DAYS ARE QUITE THE SAME
  BUT EVERY ONE OF THEM IS AN UNWINABLE GAME
  THEY START IN PAIN AND END FAR WORSE THAN
    WHEN THEY CAME
  WHAT COULD BE HARDER THAN LIFE?, OH YEAH,
  WHAT COULD BE HARDER THAN…?

  YOUR SADNESS HAS SWALLOWED THE AIR
  BUT I'M STILL BREATHING, DESPITE YOUR DESPAIR
  I DON'T UNDERSTAND YOU, I DON'T UNDERSTAND
  DON'T YOU KNOW MY HEART IS JUST A BIRD IN
    YOUR HAND…?
TRIGORIN. *(Interrupting, gently…)* You wrote that?

MASH. Last night. Well, finished it...
TRIGORIN. Really? Even with / everything...?
MASH. What did you expect? Keening?
TRIGORIN. But you're not... I mean, he's not *your*... I mean—
MASH. No. Never. But if he'd succeeded in his ridiculous—if Conrad had succeeded in killing himself I would've followed him straight into the mouth of hell. Don't... don't you dare *smile* at me, you arrogant prick, *he's my person.* I could save him. I *could.* Even if he can't see that, and never— But whatever. Doesn't matter.
TRIGORIN. Doesn't matter?
MASH. I'll marry Dev and then the worst of it will be over.
TRIGORIN. Wait, what? You'll marry Dev? Conrad's... odd friend?
MASH. Sure.
TRIGORIN. Really?
MASH. Maybe.
TRIGORIN. Ummm... *why?*
MASH. He's a good person. He's kind to animals and children. And he always smells like clean sheets...
TRIGORIN. Well, that makes perfect sense, then...
(Beat.)
MASH. To love with all your heart and know that it will never, ever be returned. *(In equal, painful balance...)* And to be loved by someone else whose love you cannot possibly return, even if he were the last man standing. What kind of a God needs a laugh that bad? *(Beat.)* Fucker.
TRIGORIN. Who, me?
MASH. God.
TRIGORIN. Ah.
MASH. What a fucker, you know? Things are so massively *fucked* down here, and he just seems to be kickin' back, laughing his ass off. I swear I can hear him sometimes, just chortling away, munching on some... celestial buttered popcorn or whatever, and watching us bounce around our pain-laced little lives as the world slips ever-closer to the cosmic crapper.
TRIGORIN. Wow. That's... / *bleak.*
MASH. *True.*
("Bleak" and "true" overlap, obscuring both...)
TRIGORIN. What's that?
MASH. *True.* That was the word you were looking for. Accurate. Insightful. *True.*

43

TRIGORIN. Well...

MASH. C'mon, it's just you and me here. You know what I mean. I've read your fucking stories. Bleakness all tied up with a pretty pink bow, that's your best trick, isn't it? C'mon, look me in the eye and tell me you don't feel the exact same way. Late at night. All alone... (If you're ever alone...)

TRIGORIN. Feel *which* way... exactly?

MASH. That we're cosmically screwed. That God is dead... or *otherwise engaged*... or... and our "leaders," so-called—even the really well-meaning ones, even those we think we love—are really errant fucking knaves or dangerously self-serving pricks, all of them, drunk with power and riches and wielding sway with a a a an arrogant hypocrisy beyond the power of poets to name... That the whole fucking game has been bought and sold a dozen times to the highest bidders... and that finally, here at civilization's eleventh hour, the course towards destruction has actually been set—like that self-destruct mechanism on the *Enterprise*—and the red light's flashing, and the siren's blaring, and we've all been warned, but—here's the thing—we just don't know how long the timer is set for...! So we all go prancing along pretending to be oblivious and blithely clocking in and having kids and paying our bills and meanwhile...

*"The sluggish economy" blah blah blah and and "the terrorist threat" blah blah blah and and and and "the refugee crisis" and "the guns" and and and "climate change" and "the war on drugs" and "the war on poverty" and "the war on women" and the war on *blah* and the war on *blah* and the war on blah blah blah blah fucking fucking blah...!*

TRIGORIN. Are you...?

MASH. I'm fine. *(Breath. Breath.)* I'm *fine.* And the fucking irony is, no matter how *inconceivably broken* the world gets, all most of us really care about, deep down, is if we get to snuggle up to someone late at night who will just maybe, just *maybe, help us to forget everything we actually know.*
(Beat. Beat...) You know what I mean. I know you know...

TRIGORIN. *(An admission.)* I do...

MASH. Thought so. I can see it. You're as lost as me. Lost in life. And dismally disappointed that this. is. it.

TRIGORIN. *(Jotting it down.)* Dismally disappointed. That's good...

MASH. Eugchh. Artists.

DEV. *(Knocking. From outside...)* Mash?

MASH. *(Under her breath.)* Oh, God...

DEV. Hello?

MASH. Come in!

DEV. Hi. *(He comes in. He wears an absurd coat and hat of some kind. Seeing Doyle.)* Oh, hi. *(To Mash.)* I got you those pecans you wanted. For the pie.

MASH. Oh, right. Thanks. I'll take 'em.

DEV. Great. *(He hands her a bag of pecans.)* Do you... need anything else?

MASH. No, thanks... Thanks.

DEV. Okay. I'm heading out. *(He starts to go. Then...)* Oh, hey, I saw a whole family of geese on the way home. Just walking along in a straight little line, right down the middle of the road. Right out there in the world, you know? Just like... *(He gently imitates the boldly walking geese...)* It was so odd. And sweet, kind of... It took my breath away, a little...

MASH. And?

DEV. Nothing. I just... Never mind. See you tomorrow. *(He leaves. Beat...)*

TRIGORIN. *(Getting up to go. It's late...)* Well, good luck with that, then...

MASH. *(Not negatively...)* Go fuck yourself.

TRIGORIN. Good night.

MASH. *(As he leaves...)* Gosh, you take everything I say so literally... *(Maybe Trigorin laughs as he leaves... Mash sits a moment. Then sings...)*

> NO TWO DAYS ARE QUITE THE SAME
> BUT EVERY ONE OF THEM IS AN UNWINABLE GAME
> THEY START IN PAIN AND END FAR WORSE THAN
>   WHEN THEY CAME
> WHAT COULD BE HARDER THAN LIFE?, OH YEAH,
> WHAT COULD BE HARDER THAN...?

16. Hi

Con enters. His head is bandaged. He sees Mash...

CON. Hey.
MASH. Hi.
(Neither can imagine what to say to the other, so they just... don't. They stand there a moment... and then he goes and starts to make himself a smoothie. She watches him awhile. She probably considers all the possible courses of behavior. Then... leaves. There can be no music during this. The hum of the refrigerator? He breathes easier once she is gone. And goes on making his smoothie...)

17. Failure

Emma enters the kitchen and sees her son. It's about 11 P.M. or so. The tension is thick between them. Charged. Volatile. Years of unspoken frustrations in both directions lurk just below the surface. They both feel misunderstood. They both feel hurt by the other. They both feel deep anger and shame and resentment. And real love. These are dangerous and deeply combustible ingredients...

EMMA. Oh.
CON. Hi.
EMMA. You're... eating...
CON. Yeah, well...
EMMA. Oh, Connie, Connie, / what am I going to do with you?
CON. Please, mother, don't...
EMMA. Why? Why, Connie, why / did you do this—
CON. Don't. Please. Anything but that.
EMMA. All right.

CON. Please?
EMMA. I said all right…
Are you going to do it again?
CON. Of course not.
EMMA. Good.
Is there anything I can—
CON. No. Can we just… *not.*
EMMA. Fine.
CON. *(To us.)* The only thing worse than trying to kill yourself and failing is having to talk to your mom after trying to kill yourself and failing—particularly when she knows deep down somewhere it's at least partially her fault, but her mouth and brain have never actually formed the phrase "I'm sorry" in her entire life, so here you are, with nothing but a berry smoothie between you, and… and…
EMMA. Nina's here.
CON. Still?
EMMA. She's worried about you.
CON. Yeah, sure…
EMMA. She is. She said she might sleep on the couch…
CON. Oh, God, really…? She brought me soup. Like she was my grandmother…
(Almost a throw-away.) Like a fucking consolation prize…
EMMA. *(Quick beat… doing the math…)* Consolation for what?
CON. *(Quick beat.)* Never mind.
(To her, gently, lovingly…) Mother, would you change my bandage?
(There is the briefest of hesitations…)
Never mind.
EMMA. No no no, of course, if you want me to…
CON. No, no, it's fine. Uncle did it not that long ago, I'm sure it's fine.
EMMA. Connie, if you want / me to change it I—
CON. It's no big deal, I don't want you to get your hands all… *bloody. (Tense beat…)*
EMMA. You're sure?
CON. I'm fine.
EMMA. *(Going to him…)* Oh, Conrad, you're going to be the death of me… I mean…
CON. …
EMMA. Thank God you missed. I would have felt just terrible if—

CON. Do you really love him?

EMMA. Of course.

CON. And you trust him?

EMMA. I do. Why?

CON. Can't you see... what he's like?

EMMA. I trust him to be *who he is*. You don't understand I love him totally, and I wouldn't want him any other way. *(Beat.)* What do you mean "what he's like"?

CON. He's a condescending, self-centered—

EMMA. That's enough!

CON. He thinks he's some kind of genius, but / he's just a third rate—

EMMA. You don't understand him! He *is* a genius! A truly great artist! You can't begin to understand / who he is and how he—

CON. No! Of course not! How could I understand a great genius?

EMMA. Oh, please!

CON. How can a failure like me possibly understand / Trigorin's *greatness*?!?

EMMA. Oh, grow up, Connie, grow up / for Christ's sake!

CON. He's probably out there right now, smarming all over Nina, convincing her / how brilliant he is—

EMMA. Oh, don't be ridiculous!

CON. Then don't be blind! He can't take his fucking eyes off her!

EMMA. Oh, don't you / DARE—

CON. How stupid can you be? And how the fuck can you fall for the exact same kind of shitty, arrogant assholes over and over and over / and over—

EMMA. You're delusional!

CON. And you're an idiot!

EMMA. And you're FUCKING IMPOSSIBLE!!!

CON. AND YOU'RE THE WORST MOTHER IN THE WORLD!!!!!

EMMA. That's better! / Very mature!

CON. I can't stand you and your men and your acting / and your—

EMMA. And I can't stand to see how pathetic you've become!

CON. You bitch!

EMMA. Failure!

CON. Whore!

EMMA. HOW DARE YOU?!?! You have no idea / what I gave up for you! What I had to sacrifice—

CON. She doesn't love me anymore!!! Don't you understand that, she DOESN'T LOVE ME ANYMORE! She is everything to me and all she can see is HIM and his fucking genius and his fucking fame and his fucking *moustache* and / his fucking clever talk and his fucking rich successful...
EMMA. Oh, Connie, Connie, Connie, I'm so, so sorry for you...
CON. Oh, God, Mama, I am so unhappy. I am so, so, so unhappy all the time...
EMMA. Oh my poor boy...
CON. *(Breaking down.)* She sees what you see now: a loser. A fucking loser...
EMMA. Oh, you're not a loser. You aren't. And of course she still loves you.
CON. Not anymore...
EMMA. You can be wonderful.
CON. ...
EMMA. You are *my son*, and you will do great things. You just need to...
CON. What?
EMMA. We'll leave tomorrow. I'll take him away, and she'll love you again. She's probably just... *dazzled.* He has a way of... I don't know... *getting in there.*
CON. Oh, God, I have to go... *(He begins to try to leave...)*
EMMA. We'll go. We'll leave, and then she'll love you again...
CON. I can't... I'm... I'm going... I'm going for a walk. *(He bolts.)*
EMMA. Connie, wait, don't walk away, stay here and— *(He is gone...)* Oh, my poor boy. Oh, my poor darling...

18. You Never Know...

A moment or two passes. Sorn enters the kitchen. Con has just passed him in the hall. He and Emma look at each other a long moment...

SORN. How is he?
EMMA. How the fuck should I know? Sad. Sad and lost. You

49

remember that play he was in the third grade where he was in that… little boat, wearing that ridiculous hat?

SORN. Yes, actually. You saw that?

EMMA. I did. I remember he looked so little up there, so… lost at sea. I just keep remembering that today… His head is fine, though, right?

SORN. It's a scratch. A few stitches. He might have thought he wanted to do it, but something in him knew better.

EMMA. Yes. *(Beat.)*

SORN. I'm worried / that he's—

EMMA. *(Heading to bed…)* Well, I'm exhausted. *(Missing what he said…)* I'm sorry?

SORN. Nothing.

EMMA. Okay. *(Heading out…)* Have you seen Doyle?

SORN. No. He was writing on the porch earlier…

EMMA. Ah. And Nina's still here?

SORN. Bedding down on the old red couch with Franny…

EMMA. Ah, Franny. That cat is such a little tramp…

SORN. Any warm body in a storm…

EMMA. Yes. Yes, indeed… And you're okay, right?

SORN. *(Beat.)* Of course. You know / me…

EMMA. All right. Good night then.

SORN. Good night.

(She goes. He takes various implements out of various cupboards and drawers and makes a delicious and unique cocktail during all this to take to his room… He should go easily and rapidly about his work, the routine casualness of his preparations undercutting the complexity and pain of what he is talking about…)

I'm a doctor. My job is to help people feel better. Ironic. When I feel so entirely shitty myself most of the time. Not that they know that. Not my sister. Not my poor, screwed-up nephew… Not my patients or my friends or my ex-wives or… you know… anyone, really.

There is so much love in this house. Or what passes for love. "If only she…" or "Why won't he…" or "What can I do…" and the like. It matters so much to them. And I get that. It mattered to me, once, too. I had my dreams. Some came true, even. But they don't know that. They never ask. I have some memories, though. Some doozies. Remember—if you take nothing else away from this… "play," or whatever it is, remember this—when you see an old

50

guy... *You Never Know.* Where he might have been. Or what he might have done. Or with whom.
Or with *whoms*... You never know.
Poor Connie. He's *in it* now. Right in the thick of it... Can't see the edge of the forest in any direction. I remember the feeling. Awful. And *wonderful*...
(He starts cleaning up, maybe...) But here's the thing. I get up most mornings around dawn or so. It's still dark, and often still cold. And I'm alone. And I shave and shower and get dressed, and the last thing I do before I leave the house is brush my teeth. And three mornings out of five, I wonder—while I'm brushing my teeth, for some reason, always right then, in the midst of this most mundane of morning ablutions—I wonder... Why go on? Why walk out the door and into the day and do... all the things I do. And you know why I do it?
Do you? Do you? *(Good if he gets them to say "no"...)*
Nor do I, my friends. Nor do I...
(He leaves. Lights shift. Perhaps, if the radio is on, it shifts to another tune, another tone. It is now clearly later, the middle of the night. Maybe 3 A.M.?)

19. Undone

Trigorin enters, maybe singing softly to himself, and starts meticulously making a peanut butter and jam sandwich. Or eating an apple. Or... He periodically looks at the door to the kitchen, expectantly... Nina, scantily clad on the couch, is acutely with him throughout this. Maybe there is some time here, or maybe he pops in and starts speaking to us right away...

TRIGORIN. So, you know, people ask me all the time... what's my secret? How do I *understand* them so well? How can I know their inmost secrets when I've never even met them, and the like. And I think the simple truth is... *I love them.* All of them. And by "them," I mean, of course, *you*. All of you. You're all so fucked up

in such endlessly fascinating ways that I can't help but love you. And if you love someone you want to *know* them, "*get*" them, get *inside* them... so to speak. *(The sound of a cat elsewhere in the house... He looks at the doorway. Beat...)*
What gets just a little bit tricky is—
(Nina enters gently... She knows he is here. She has been waiting, hoping, not sure if he would come down, not sure if she would have the chance, not sure if she would take it if she did, not sure she will go all the way through with it even when they are both in the quiet, late-night, gently humming kitchen...)
NINA. Hello.
TRIGORIN. Hello...
NINA. Hi.
TRIGORIN. Pajamas.
NINA. I couldn't sleep.
TRIGORIN. Neither could I.
NINA. Oh. Why couldn't you sleep?
TRIGORIN. Oh I don't sleep that much, really. Four, five hours a night, if I'm lucky.
I'm... quintessentially restless. Why couldn't *you* sleep?
NINA. *(Somehow flirtatiously...)* Oh...
TRIGORIN. Insomnia?
NINA. No.
TRIGORIN. Bad dreams?
NINA. No.
TRIGORIN. A pea?
NINA. Umm, no, I didn't have to—
TRIGORIN. No no no... a pea. *(Showing the shape and size of the object...)*
NINA. *(Getting it.)* Ah, got it. No, I'm no princess...
TRIGORIN. An unsettling nocturnal desire, then, to, ummm... to "end the heartache and the thousand natural shocks the flesh is heir to"?
NINA. Not so much. *(Quick beat. Finding this in the moment. A sudden inspiration, as it were—a sudden, odd, smart way in...)* It was more the next line, I think.
TRIGORIN. The next...?
NINA. Yes.
(He mumbles through the speech. "And by a sleep to say"... "flesh is heir to..." to find the next line... Gets it.)

TRIGORIN. A consummation devoutly to be wished?

NINA. That's the one.

TRIGORIN. *(Hearing that first word...) Oh.*

NINA. That's why I couldn't sleep.

TRIGORIN. Because...

NINA and TRIGORIN. *(Bold, slow, and direct.)* Because of a consummation devoutly to be wished.

TRIGORIN. *(Getting it in no uncertain terms...)* Oh, my...

NINA. *(Moving forward, pushing past what she has just put in the room. But both are acutely aware that that energy is now absolutely mounting in the room...)* Have you ever wondered if he was asking the right question?

TRIGORIN. Who?

NINA. Hamlet.

TRIGORIN. Which question?

NINA. To be or not to be. I don't think that's really The Question at all.

TRIGORIN. Oh no? Then what's the question?

NINA. To act or not to act. To do, or leave undone. And speaking of undone... *(She begins to advance towards him, slowly, gently un-done-ing herself...)*

TRIGORIN. *(Amazed and delighted and aghast...)* Who are you?

NINA. *(Shrugging off her pajama top or T-shirt. She stands there, topless...)* I'm the one with the perfect breasts, remember.

TRIGORIN. Oh, yes, yes...

NINA. If you want them, they're yours. If you want me, I'm yours. If you want my life, now or ever, it's yours and yours and always, only yours...

TRIGORIN. Oh, Nina... *(He moves towards her, perhaps touches her, perhaps kisses her, perhaps, perhaps, perhaps... Emma suddenly appears from somewhere.)*

20. Terrible to Behold

EMMA. *(Smiling, grand and terrifying all at once... She is not surprised. You have the sense she has seen or sensed or something...)* Well hello there, darling.

NINA. Oh, God!

EMMA. Oh, no, not *God*, child, but still… full of wrath and terrible to behold.

TRIGORIN. Emma—

EMMA. Shut up, my love. Nina…?

NINA. Yes?

EMMA. Leave.

NINA. What?

EMMA. Leave. *Now.*

NINA. Oh.

EMMA. And not just the room, *you traitor*, the house. The hemisphere, if possible.

NINA. All right. *(She starts out…)*

EMMA. And Nina? *(Nina turns.)* Don't ever come near me or any of my men ever again, or I will quite simply kill you until you are utterly and entirely dead. Okay? Okay. *(Nina turns to go. Emma calls, pseudo-friendly.)* Good night…!

NINA. *(Turning sharply to Trigorin before she goes.)* Remember what I said.

EMMA. GO!!!

21. Let Me Go

Nina is gone. Emma and Trigorin stand there for several moments, perhaps, transfixed. They stare at each other, neither one quite willing or able to speak first, to begin. Who will speak first? What will they say? After some time…

TRIGORIN. Let me go.

EMMA. *(Amazed.)* What?

TRIGORIN. Let me go.

EMMA. No. *(Beat.)*

TRIGORIN. Let me go.

EMMA. Never.

TRIGORIN. Let me go.

(… And with that, her performance for him begins. It is real, true,

grounded, absolutely high-stakes, but a performance but a consummate performer nonetheless...)

EMMA. Am I so *old*, so *ugly* that you can stand there and speak to me like that?

TRIGORIN. Let me go.

EMMA. I won't! I won't let you throw yourself away!! I won't let you destroy your happiness and mine, and my son's, and hers, too, (the little bitch!), and all for nothing. She's a girl! A stupid, stupid, stupid *girl*. She has nothing for you!

TRIGORIN. Let me go.

EMMA. Over my dead body. *(Beat.)*

TRIGORIN. Let me go.

EMMA. No.

You're an amazing man, a great artist, your best work is still ahead of you and I can't bear to see you throw it all away. We both know what will happen. Think! Use your fucking head for one moment instead of your aging dick. *(She slaps him hard.)* Think! Imagine. You will run after her. Burning. Blazing with need. Like a jackel. Like a forest fire! Like a *man*! The chase! The adventure! The triumph! The conquering hero! Good for you, look what you can do: You can astonish a girl with a daddy complex!!! Well done, you! And now you have her. And it is wonderful. Luscious. Delicious. *Uncomplicated. For hours and hours and hours...*

Maybe days.

And then??? And then what?

Play it out to the end, my love. It's a dead end. Unreal. Empty. Not something you can live in, not really. It's an illusion of something— an imitation of something you wanted when you were fifteen and could never have then because you were odd and pimply and unpopular so you desperately want it now.

But wake up! Think!

Escape is not for you.

Or for me.

We Are Artists, for fuck's sake, and we need to be right in the middle of *life*, of *living*, of *raw reality*. Let ordinary everyday men be run by their fears and their pricks and their desperate attempts to stave off mortality... but not a Great Artist like you. Not you! Not an Actual Man. *(He is teetering... She goes to him as she speaks and perhaps she undoes his robe, letting it fall to the floor. Or not. Whatever makes sense... Perhaps he is naked underneath. He stands*

there…) I *see you.* I *know you.* ALL of you. No one will ever know you like I do and you know it. You know it in your bones. Look at me. I am here. I am real. *(She drops her robe as well, perhaps. Or not. If so, she stands there, naked before him. If not… metaphorically naked.)* Do you hear me?
I LOVE YOU FOR WHO YOU ARE.
For everything you truly are in the world. And I am REAL. A *real* mirror. A *complicated* mirror! Not the fun house mirror of youth and wishing. And I will love you forever and ever without end…
Now Come Back to My Bed. And never leave it again.
(They kiss, passionately, deeply… They perhaps remain in some manner of passionate sexual engagement throughout the entire following scene…)

22. Late Night Quartet

Conrad and Dev, Nina and Mash enter. Eventually Sorn also enters and he watches what transpires. Trigorin and Emma, oblivious, continue… At some point Sorn enters into this world, in it but also separate from it…

CON and DEV. It's impossible!
NINA and MASH. It's unfair!
NINA, MASH, CON, and DEV. Love is IMPOSSIBLE!!!
CON and DEV. The thing is, the thing is this, the thing is…
NINA and MASH. …it's not my *fault*, it's *not*,
It's not my *choice*…!

CON. She hates me in this	DEV. I love her in this one
one particular way:	very particular way:

NINA and MASH. The heart just… *does things*!
It just DOES things, it just does…
CON. I DISAPPOINT HER!
DEV. I WORSHIP HER!
NINA and MASH. … all these *things*…!
CON and DEV. It's that simple!
NINA and MASH. I have these dreams,
These *relentless, raging* dreams,

These Stupid Fucking Dreams of Perfect Love!

CON and DEV. I get it, I do, I really do, she doesn't *hate* me...

MASH and NINA. No no no, not *perfect*, not not not...

CON. But I sure do DISAPPOINT her!

DEV. But I sure do BOTHER her!

MASH and NINA. It's just...

CON and DEV. I see it in her eyes...

MASH and NINA. It's just...

CON and DEV. I read it on her lips...

MASH and NINA. It's just...

CON and DEV. I feel it in my balls...

She wants something that is JUST NOT ME!

MASH and NINA. I want something that is JUST NOT HIM!

MASH and NINA. I'm sorry, I'm sorry, I'm so, so, so, so, so, so sorry...

CON and DEV. Love is AWFUL.

NINA and MASH. Love is ABSURD.

NINA, MASH, CON, and DEV. Love is SO FUCKING UNFAIR!!!

CON. The thing is...

MASH. What sucks is...

DEV. What's tricky is...

NINA. What's hard is...

MASH. *(Simultaneously.)* I don't know if I should just live in endless, stupid clueless *hope* and *anger* and *pain and sadness*, or if I should tear this love out by the roots, just rip it out by the fucking roots and hope that something else, something new will grow in the twisted, ripped-up hole in my chest where this love used to grow.

NINA. *(Simultaneously.)* Even if this is real, even if, even if all that I've ever ever ever dreamed of lies arrayed before me like candy on a a a carpet or a feast for my longing, hopeful heart, can I really build a new love on the ruins of an old, comfortable, kind, childish, child-like love which is all I've ever really known?

CON. *(Simultaneously.)* Who hates me? Who up there, somewhere, hates me so fucking much that I have all this HUGE, HARD, RIDICULOUS STUFF running around inside of me, all these fierce fucking *feelings* and *needs* and *insights* and I don't have the fucking talent to express them or the power or or or or whatever to do what needs to be done.

DEV. *(Simultaneously.)* I'm a good person, a kind person, I'm trying my hardest, I'm trying to do the right thing all the time, pretty much, all the time, and I think I have a lot to give—and *get*, I'm not a saint—but I somehow I feel like I should get a chance to just… give what I've got to give.

NINA, MASH, CON, and DEV. I am FLAWED!

I have NEEDS!!

I WANT MORE!!!

CON. It's not / my fault

DEV. It's not / my fault

NINA. It's not / my fault

MASH. It's not / my fault

NINA, MASH, CON, and DEV. IT'S NOT MY FUCKING FAULT!!!

CON.	MASH.	DEV.	NINA.
And yet…	And yet…	And yet…	And yet…

SORN. So much feeling…

End of Act Two

ACT THREE

23. On and On

Lights. The stage is perhaps much as it was for the first act. Also different. Decorations for a party. Mash and Dev are onstage. Con is, too, but in the background. Lounging? Smoking? Setting up party decorations? Drinking, more than likely. He is not in good psychological shape and should never be fully on top of his game, not any time in this entire act. He is truly Not Doing Well. He is on edge, someone you would worry about... Mash has her ukulele. Dev plays bass, or another uke, or glockenspiel, or something. They're dressed for a party.

DEV. *(To the audience.)* We wrote this song. Together.
MASH. *(Not unkindly.)* If we're going to sing it, let's just sing it, okay?
DEV. Okay. *(To us.)* It's about... life. *(Making a big inclusive gesture to include All of Life, maybe...)* About *life*, you know?
MASH. C'mon. They'll get it or they won't. Play...
DEV. Okay. *(They start to play... Gently, to us, teasing Mash.)* Don't judge...
MASH. *(To Dev. Not without affection...)* Shut up.
    WHEN YOU'RE JUST COOKIN'
    WHEN YOU'RE NOT LOOKIN' FOR A CHANGE,
    IT'S STRANGE,
    HOW HEARTS AND MINDS CAN REARRANGE
    SUCH AN ODD EXCHANGE...
    WHEN LIFE HAPPENS

    WHEN YOU'RE NOT TRYIN'
    WHEN YOU'RE JUST CRYIN' ON THE STAIR
    IT'S NOT FAIR
    THE WAY THE ACT OF SIMPLY BREATHING AIR

CAN BE HARD TO BEAR
BUT THEN LIFE HAPPENS…
MASH and DEV.
AND ON AND ON AND ON WE GO
AND ON AND ON AND ON DAYS FLOW
LONELY, LOVELY, RICH AND ROUGH
ALL TOO MUCH… AND NEVER ENOUGH, ON
AND ON
DEV.
WHILE YOUR CHILD'S SLEEPIN'
WHILE THE WILLOW'S WEEPIN' IN THE YARD
IT'S HARD
TO MAKE IT THROUGH A SINGLE DAY UNMARRED
OR UNSCARRED…
BUT LIFE JUST HAPPENS
DEV and MASH.
NOW THAT YOU'VE STARTED,
THOUGH YOU'VE BEEN THWARTED, TRY AGAIN
TO BEGIN
EVERY SINGLE DAY AS THOUGH YOU'RE GONNA
WIN
YOU HOPE AGAIN…
BUT THEN LIFE HAPPENS…

AND ON AND ON AND ON WE GO
AND ON AND ON AND ON DAYS FLOW
LONELY, LOVELY, RICH AND ROUGH
ALL TOO MUCH… AND NEVER ENOUGH, ON
AND ON
ALL TOO MUCH… AND NEVER ENOUGH, ON
AND ON
ALL TOO MUCH… AND NEVER ENOUGH, ON
AND ON
MASH. I'm gonna check on the cake.
(Mash gets up, kisses Dev quite sweetly, and heads off…)
DEV. Great.
(She leaves. He watches her walk off, loving her…)

24. Thwarted

DEV. *(Turns to us.)* It's four years later. *(Being very clear...)* Everything that happened in the first two acts... happened four years ago now.
CON. *(From the background. He does not listen to Dev for most of the following. He is in a weird fucking mood, kind of manic, kind of despairing, rambling a bit... What people used to call a "devil may care" attitude perhaps... past caring... Referring to the line in the song:)* "You've been thwarted," huh?
DEV. How's that?
CON. Thwarted. I like that word. Thwarted.
DEV. Let me catch you up...
CON. "Drats, thwarted again."
DEV. *(To us.)* Trigorin left here with Emma—you know, back then—but then Nina just disappeared a few days later. And the next thing we knew... they were together. An "item," or whatever.
CON. Thwart. Thwart.
DEV. Conrad took it all pretty hard, as you can imagine.
CON. *(Trying it out, almost under his breath...)* "I will thwart you."
DEV. Nina's kind of a famous actress now. Some stage. Movies. Or *a* movie. Mostly TV. Crime shows, I'm told. Testifying about bad things bad men have done to her. Breaking down in tears a lot. She's... you know... *(Whispering so Con won't hear.)* not so good. Not terrible, just...
CON. "Why are you thwarting me?" *(A toss-away, imitating an ingénue in a melodrama, perhaps, or Blanche DuBois, or...)* "And here in public..."
DEV. Trigorin "opened doors" for her, I guess.
CON. Thwart.
DEV. He wrote the movie, I think. Or maybe it was another movie he wrote she was almost in. Or something. I have a hard time... *caring*, I guess.
Then after about a year they had a baby, and then lost it after just a few weeks. So awful. I mean I honestly can't imagine anything worse... If we lost one of our kids I can't—oh, right. "Our kids." Yeah, well, Mash and I are married now.
Yeah, I know. I was surprised as you are. If you're totally shocked,

that is. She finally... gave in, I guess. Not quite the romantic ideal of one's foolish youth, but still... I'm genuinely grateful. Usually. You know. Life is still life, right? Even when you amazingly *get* the girl, there are still... *things*. Don't you find?

Anyway...

CON. Thwart thwart thwart thwart thwart.

DEV. We have three kids already. Coralie is twenty-two months today, and the twins, Malachi and Merlin, are just eleven weeks. They look almost exactly like me. I don't think she can quite believe it. But life life life, right?

CON. After a while the word makes no sense.

DEV. Conrad still lives here at home.

CON. Thwart. Thwart. Thwart.

DEV. Writing. And drinking. In tandem, as it were. The tortured artist blah blah blah...

Which brings us, perhaps, to today. Which is shaping up to be a doozy.

Dr. Sorn turns sixty today—he's lookin' a little rocky if you ask me, but I don't know, maybe he's just worried about Con... or maybe it's... you know... *parties*. Or this particular party... 'Cause Emma and Trigorin are coming. Oh, yeah, they're back together, for maybe a year now. And, you know, just as icing for the proverbial cake, Nina is back in town, too, this week. Not for the party. Staying with her fucked up folks and resting. You know... "resting."

CON. *(A bit more loudly now...)* It sounds like really bad art. "How was the show?"

"It thwarted. It fucking thwarted..."

DEV. *(Finally forced to engage with him...)* Are you being thwarted?

CON. What?

DEV. You feeling thwarted?

CON. By?

DEV. How should I know? Love. Life. Your mom. Art.

CON. Don't *you*?

DEV. What?

CON. Feel thwarted.

DEV. By?

CON. All of it! The total... *tonnage* of it all. The weight of all the bullshit stifling all possibility of forward movement. Power, politics, sewage, academia, art... It's all the same and it's all fucked. Yeah, I feel thwarted. Good and thwarted!

DEV. By...?

CON. THEM! OLD PEOPLE! Old, rich, successful, selfish, wealthy white people.

Who do you think? Even the lovely, well-meaning ones! They got here first, found a feast, ate it, and left us scraps... or not even scraps, mostly. They just fucking ate the feast. They ate it. And now they're leaving us the bill.

DEV. Wow, you *really* hate him, don't you?

CON. Who?

DEV. Trigorin.

CON. I'm not talking about him!

DEV. Yes you are. You always are. When you're mad about anything, it's really just him. When you hate "rich, white, successful people," you can tell yourself anything you want, but you're just talking about him.

CON. Bullshit.

DEV. Okay. But...

CON. What?

DEV. Nothing.

CON. No, what?

DEV. Well... I mean... I'm sorry, but he just stole your girlfriend, you know? I mean, that totally sucks, but that was years ago now, and—

CON. It's not just him! It's all of them! They've stolen our future! Can't you see that?

DEV. Not really, no. Wait! Newsflash... This just in... *(Listening to a newsflash over the wire!)* "Human Beings Take As Much As They Can Get." Con, this is fascinating. It seems we're motivated by "greed" and "a desire for comfort" and therefore sometimes take more than we need. This is amazing...!

CON. You honestly don't think they've mortgaged our future?

DEV. How the hell should I know? I get up each morning, put on my pants, and try to get through my day. That's about what I got in me these days.

CON. *(Dark and twisty...)* Yeah, I don't even get that far half the time...

DEV. Have a small gaggle of kids. That'll get you going in the morning...

CON. Yeah, there's an idea. I'd be a great dad, don't you think???

DEV. Yeah, no, you'd suck, but... they're amazing teachers.

CON. Teachers? Seriously?

DEV. Seriously.

CON. You call them the Poop-A-Matics. Mash calls them the Insatiables. You've both given your children terrible *band names*, but somehow—

DEV. Come babysit Cora sometime. Watch her sleep. Listen to her snotty breathing through those impossibly tiny nostrils... or let her wrap her whole hand around your finger... Maybe she'll figure it all out, you know? Or one of the twins. Save the world. Invent a... helpful thing.

CON. Yeah, well, that sounds great and all, but—

DEV. *(Bottom-line.)* Try loving something more than yourself. *(This pulls Con up short...)* I'm just sayin'. It does something to you. Something worthwhile.

CON. Oh, for fuck's sake, Dev, are you kidding me? *(Simple, true, totally bottom-line...)* I love almost everything more than myself. *(This pulls Dev up short. That was not the way that was supposed to go...)* Why won't Nina even see me?

DEV. Oh, Connie...

CON. And what the fuck are they doing here? Is she trying to torture me?

DEV. She's here because—

CON. I know why she's here! But from whence does he get the fucking nerve?

DEV. Well, yeah, that. That does make me want to just kick him in the balls.

CON. Good. I'm glad. Don't hold back on my account...

25. Feelings

The party pours onstage. They've been drinking. Sorn is in a high rare mood, pushing buttons, instigating… Con steps to the edge and does his best to stay there. Trigorin is aware of the dicey complexity of the situation and is trying to be… careful. Emma is doing her best to make it all seem fine and normal…

EMMA. *(Mid-funny story…)* … but she couldn't—I swear to God—she *couldn't* walk *like a human being.* We were all *aghast.* I mean, there we are, trying to act with this… blonde Southern Kewpie doll… and… I mean, with tits like those I'm not saying she needs to be *Daniel Day-Lewis*, or even even even…
DEV. *Julianne Moore*?
EMMA. *(She hears him. But going on…)* Good. Or even *good.* But still… The arms swing opposite from the legs when human beings walk. I have found. And I swear, as God is my witness, she could. not. do it. She was all… *(She walks with her left leg and arm and right leg and arm in tandem, moving forward and back at the same time, awkwardly…)*
I had to beg the director to put her out of our misery.
MASH. You had her fired?
EMMA. What? Oh, yes, I had to, sweetie, she was ruining the movie…
DEV. Wow.
TRIGORIN. Movies are tricky.
SORN. Are they?
TRIGORIN. *I* think so.
SORN. What do you think, Conrad? Are you finding that *plays* are tricky?
CON. I don't know.
TRIGORIN. Oh, right, of course, they're / doing your—
CON. It's not a big deal.
TRIGORIN. But it's happening?
CON. Yeah.
TRIGORIN. When?

CON. Now.

TRIGORIN. That's wonderful… Why aren't you there?

CON. I was. For a while…

DEV. *(Keeping it light.)* Like three days… *(Con shrugs or walks away, or…)*

MASH. He doesn't want to get caught up in "the bullshit."

TRIGORIN. Sorry?

MASH. The bullshit. Of "The Theatre."

TRIGORIN. Ah.

EMMA. Which bullshit is that?

CON. I'm sorry?

EMMA. I'm just curious… in your experience… what is it that you are calling "bullshit"?

TRIGORIN. Please don't…   SORN. Emma…

CON. No, it's fine.

The ego, mostly. The Parade of Ego. That's what I am calling "bullshit."

EMMA. But darling, you / can't let…

CON. One of the actresses' nicknames was "What About *Me?*" That was her *nickname.* She answered to that. "Where's 'What About *Me*'"? "Oh, sorry, I was reading my own press…" It made me kinda sick…

EMMA. Yes, well we can't / all be…

SORN. Well, I think it is great that it's happening and I'm looking forward to seeing it.

TRIGORIN. Absolutely. Is it a nice theatre?

CON. *(Looking around, perhaps, at the theatre we are all in…)* It's all right.

TRIGORIN. Well, you have to start somewhere, right, Emma?

EMMA. Absolutely.

SORN. It's a wonderful script, I think. Funny and sad… and very *true… (Checking in with Con…)* It's almost a new *form* of theatre, really…

CON. *(From a distance, referencing his uncle, ironically…)* My agent.

TRIGORIN. What's it called again? I saw your mother had the script but I can't / quite recall—

MASH. *Stupid Fucking Bird.*

TRIGORIN. Ah. Right. *(Directly to Con.)* Good title.

CON. Thanks.

DEV. That'll sell some tickets.

SORN. Don't you think it's a wonderful script, Emma?

EMMA. You know, it's ridiculous, but I just haven't had the chance to read it yet. I've been so crazy...

MASH. Too bad. It's great. And there's a perfect role for you in it.

EMMA. Is there?

MASH. Yeah.

EMMA. *(Beat.)* Well, now I'm terrified...

CON. Don't be. You're unrecognizable.

EMMA. Oh?

CON. She's a *brunette*. *(Note: Not the hair color of the actress playing Emma.)*

EMMA. Ah, well then...

TRIGORIN. But you feel good about the script?

CON. Sure.

SORN. Is there a role for me? Maybe I can start a last-minute career...

CON. Absolutely. You can play the bird.

SORN. Excellent. I always wanted to do something artistic.

TRIGORIN. Did you?   EMMA. Really?

SORN. I always wanted to do just about anything other than being a fucking doctor. *(Note: He never usually swears.)* All those sick people. Uggghh!

EMMA. You've never said that before.

SORN. I've never been turning sixty before. I've never been dying before.

CON. Uncle... EMMA. Now   MASH. Don't DEV. What's
                 you promised...   talk like that...   that?

SORN. I've never told the truth about damn near anything before, if you want to know the truth / so just...

EMMA. *(Calmingly, lovingly...)* Okay, have you maybe had a bit much?

SORN. ... let me talk! I never— Let me talk.

CON.   EMMA.   TRIGORIN.
Okay...   Of course.   Certainly, certainly...

SORN. This is my party right?

EMMA. Absolutely.

SORN. And I want to ask everyone a serious question.

DEV. All right...

SORN. Do you all... feel all the feelings you say you feel? That's my question.

EMMA. Why do you ask?

SORN. It's just that I... well, I don't always feel... *authentic.*

TRIGORIN. Authentic?

SORN. I feel *make-believe.*

DEV. *(Takes in the audience. Maybe others do too...)* I think we all do...

MASH. Back in a minute... *(Mash slips out to go get the cake...)*

SORN. Most days I feel like I'm... well, like I'm *performing.* Like I'm playing a role in my own life. The role of "me."

TRIGORIN. Perhaps you'd like to switch. Want to try the role of me? I've always wanted to know what it was like to be a real doctor...

CON. Ooo! Can I?

TRIGORIN. Sorry?

CON. Can *I* switch with you?

TRIGORIN. Ummm...

CON. Just for a day, maybe? Or even an hour? 'Cause I gotta tell you, I can't help but be curious about what it'd feel like to be inside that... *fascinating* head of yours because it passes my total fucking understanding / how you can manage to—

EMMA. All right, that's enough, I'm warning you—

CON. You're warning *me?* *(Beat. Then he walks away... Awkward moment... They scatter a bit, leaving Emma and Trigorin a semi-private moment...)*

EMMA. *(Hushed, just to Trigorin.)* It's like he's still fourteen fucking years old...

TRIGORIN. *(Hushed, just to Emma.)* It's okay.

EMMA. *(Hushed, just to Trigorin.)* I want to just... *spank* him. *(Beat.)*

DEV. Well, I think we're all kind of performing every day, aren't we? In our own ways?

SORN. Are we? That's what I'm asking.

DEV. What do you mean, exactly?

SORN. I know what's expected of me. I have a sense of how I'm supposed to act given my age and job and so on, so I say the right things, or at least have the right expression on my face, mostly. But *I just don't feel all the things I pretend to feel.* I say words and make faces and even talk about feelings, sometimes. But I don't have them. I fool people. *All the people,* I think. I think you all think I feel things. But I don't feel those things. And I never have. *I never have.*

I just act like I do.

EMMA. Then maybe you should have won all those awards, not me.

Because you sure fooled the fuck out of me...

SORN. But my question is this... my question is: Is this just me? Is this just me?

Or is this what everybody does?

(Beat. Beat. Perhaps the whole cast looks out to the audience to see if that is in fact what everyone is doing... Then Mash enters with a birthday cake with lit candles, and she starts singing. Everyone eventually joins in... Or not...)

MASH.

HAPPY BIRTHDAY TO YOU

HAPPY BIRTHDAY TO YOU

HAPPY BIRTHDAY, DEAR EUGENE...

HAPPY BIRTHDAY TO YOU!

(The party disperses, leaving Con alone onstage...)

26. Not Not

Con is agitated, restless, pacing, maybe. Still drinking, too...

CON. You know what fucking sucks about a little success? It just feels like a set up for a new kind of failure. A more painful kind. Because now instead of just my family, I'll get to have, you know... perfect strangers judging and pitying me, too.

My fucking play. Not an original thought in it. It's practically a fucking love story, for fuck's sake, full of people just angsting and whining and going on and on endlessly about whatever the fuck I was thinking of at the time...

I mean, new forms? Why? *Why?* Why new forms? How about this for an idea: Just do the old forms BETTER! Who am I to change them? I mean, aren't there reasons that protagonists and antagonists and rising action and climaxes and dénouements have been around for thousands of years?

Trigorin's stories are sharp. Clean. Smart. Efficient. *(Turning to us with violence, on one breath...)* Yes, I've read them, I've read every-

thing the motherfucker's ever written pretty much, before he met my mother and after, I was lying when I told Nina I hadn't, of course I was, what do you think, my mother is fucking shacked up with a great fucking writer, maybe one of the great writers of our time and I'm just not going to read his books and stories, are you crazy?
(Finally getting to the subtext that's been burning under everything from the beginning of the act.) Nina's been here for a fucking week! A week. I went to see her. She wouldn't see me. I haven't seen her in… a long time.
I tried before. Followed her. What a fucking idiot. But I couldn't… not.
I *couldn't NOT.*
Haven't you ever *not been able to NOT*…?
It sucks.
And it's dangerous…
(Then…a knock…)

27. A Seagull

CON. Who's there?
NINA. Hello?
CON. Nina?!?
NINA. Hello?!
CON. Nina! Oh, God in Heaven. One second…
(He lets her in. Nina looks like a different person. Older, broken and with only a thin hold on reality. She slips in and out of lucidity and is given to poetry and fantasy. There is urgency behind every moment and she can never settle in any one place or on any one thought. The scene just rolls on and on and on…)
NINA. Hello Connie.
CON. Hi. Hi.
NINA. Hi. Look at you. It's *you*. It's… your face.
CON. Oh, my God, I am so glad you're here. Are you okay?
NINA. Sure, of course. Flying high…
CON. Do you need something to drink, or…?
NINA. No.
CON. You sure?

NINA. I'm fine.

CON. Okay.

NINA. Or... do you have any of those cookies? With the cream and the jelly in the middle? That your Grandbop used to give to us if we... polished things, or whatever...

CON. No. No, sorry. Jesus, I haven't thought of those in—

NINA. It's okay. No / cookies, then...

CON. I came to see you, but... I guess you / know that, right?

NINA. I'm sorry, I couldn't quite... you know...

CON. Yeah, I know. I get it.

NINA. You don't...

CON. What?

NINA. You know...

Hate me?

CON. Wow. Okay. You don't get it, do you?

NINA. Get what?

CON. I love you. Period.

I love you and I always will. Always and forever, no matter what. It's not a choice, even, it's just... you're a part of me... *structurally.* I could never see you again, ever... *ever*, and I'd still love you on / the day I die.

NINA. Oh, God, what are you saying...?

CON. Don't get me wrong I am not saying this is a good thing. It might just kill me within the hour, but I'm just telling you the fucking / truth. I'm just—

NINA. How do you not hate me? I left you. I ran away to your mother's lover. I broke everything that was ever good in the world / for my own selfish—

CON. Stop it, for fuck's sake stop it, I know what you did, I don't need a litany of sins. You're human. You're a human being. A flawed human being like the rest / of us, and—

NINA. I don't think I am.

CON. Oh, you're flawed, believe me, I mean, I love you and / always will, but—

NINA. No, I'm flawed, I am, of course I am, but I don't think I'm... what you said.

CON. What did I—?

NINA. The other thing you said.

CON. *(Thinking, not a likely answer.)* What...

A human being?

71

NINA. Yes. I don't think I'm that.

CON. Then what are you?

NINA. A seagull. A seagull. I think I'm kind of a seagull. Don't you?

CON. Nina...?

NINA. I'm not an actress. I'm not. I thought I was but... did you ever see me?

CON. Of course.

NINA. Have you ever seen anything so awful in your life?

CON. I / thought you were—

NINA. DON'T LIE TO ME!

Don't you dare lie to me, Conrad. I was there. I was right up there on that stage and I know: I am the worst actress ever. I can't say words. I don't know how to stand or use my hands. I don't... *mean anything*! I can't tell the truth for one second onstage or in front of a camera. I just can't... *act*.

You know the last time I was any good?

CON. When?

NINA. In your play. I was good in that. I had... *enthusiasm*. I had *integrity*. I was... *myself*. Am I a seagull?

CON. No.

NINA. Then why did you shoot a seagull? Wasn't that me?

CON. No. I mean, yes, kind of...

NINA. So I *am* a seagull?

CON. No. It's a...

NINA. What?

CON. A metaphor. A... symbol. I thought... Oh, God, it sounds so fucking stupid.

NINA. You thought I was *like* a seagull?

CON. Yes.

NINA. So you shot me? Why did you shoot me, if you love me? I have thought about that a thousand times. Lying in bed. Some bed. Somewhere. And suddenly I would think: "Why? Why did he shoot me?"

CON. I didn't... I mean... I love you, Nina, and I was just... just...

NINA. Yes?

CON. I have no fucking idea! It was... *art*, or something. I was trying to let you know how much I loved you and how much you meant to me.

NINA. Then you shouldn't have shot me! You shouldn't have *shot* me. You shouldn't shoot the things you love.

That should be on a T-shirt: You Shouldn't Shoot the Things You Love.

CON. Nina. Just look at me.

NINA. I'd rather not. *(Beat. Then slowly, carefully...)* Is he here?

CON. *(Knowing full well who...)* Who?

(Nina just looks at him...)

Yeah. Bastard.

NINA. He's not a bastard.

CON. No...?

NINA. No. He's the devil. A beautiful... bored... brilliant devil. How else could he have...?

Her name... her name was Hannah. And she was only little.

Her hands... were only *this* big. Her fingernails were so tiny you didn't even know how they knew they were fingernails yet... She was perfect.

A perfect little bird, and... and then one day... and then one day... *not.*

She just... *stopped.*

And then he left. Just... *left.*

It was all so, so, so *awful...*

CON. Oh, Nina, I'm so, so—

NINA. I'm a seagull, right?

CON. You need a rest. You need someone who loves you to take care of you. Let me take care of you. I can do that. I could fucking *do that...*

NINA. I leave in an hour. A new play. A lovely little play. Maybe this will be the one. Maybe this time I'll be wonderful. Radiant. Ideal.

CON. Listen...

NINA. More likely I'll be awful. Wretched. Unwatchable...

CON. Please, just let me—

NINA. *(Going right on, ignoring him...)* You know why?

CON. Nina—

NINA. You know why?!?

CON. Why?

NINA. I'm a seagull. And seagulls can't act. That should be on a T-shirt, too:

Seagulls Can't Act.

You know why?

CON. Look, Nina—

NINA. You know *why*?!?!

CON. Why?

NINA. *(Breaking down, maybe, for the first time, and really looking at her old friend and first love for the first time…)* Because they have no lips. They have no little lips to kiss you with. And they have tiny, tiny little birdlike hearts—only little tiny hearts that can't hold all the love you deserve. Seagulls can't act because they fly up above all the things that matter on this earth… all the things that are real, all those who love them and would take care of them and all their tiny babies and they are selfish and selfish and selfish and selfish and selfish… *(She breaks down and can't go on… or not… but she stops…)*

CON. *(Embracing her…)* Oh, Nina, Nina I am so sorry for everything…

NINA. I have to go. I have to go.

CON. No, you can't. Stay with me. Let me love you. Let me take care of you. I could do that. I could be really good at that. That's why I was / put here on…

NINA. *(Pulling herself together.)* I can't. I just *can't*. It is all too absurd.

CON. Wait, please—

NINA. Goodbye, Connie. Thank you. Thank you for loving me. Thank you for shooting me. I think you love me better and more than anyone ever has or ever will and I don't understand you and I never will but thank you for everything. Goodbye. *(She leaves, abruptly.)*

28. What Now?

CON. So… Here We Are. Fuck.

Fuck!!!

This is my life. My *life*!! I *tried* and I *failed*. So I tried again, and I didn't fail better, I failed *more*!!! The story of my life has been written, and the CliffsNotes version is: YOU FUCKING SUCK! Which I guess I've always known…!

(Calling offstage or to the universe…) Thanks, Mom!!!

So what now? What's the point of going on?! What's the motherfucking *point*?

My life is a fucking disaster! "Love" is a a a *shipwreck*! And my "art" has about as much chance of changing the world as fucking fucking

fucking... *CONGRESS! (Suddenly and sharply to the audience.)* What the fuck are you laughing at? Is this funny to you? Enjoying my pain? Do you have any idea what happens next? Do you? Well, for those of you not so well versed in nineteenth century Russian drama, this is where I die. Yep, that's right, campers, I *die*. Anguished tears. Burn my manuscripts. Despair despair despair... Gunshot! And then you cry. You *CRY*. Or wake up. Or whatever...

And then stand up, give a quick little thumbs up or down or non-committal shrug to whoever you're here with, and then whip out your phone to check your missed calls and texts before you've even sidled to the end of your fucking row! This is where the play ends, I'm fucking dead, Nina's shithouse crazy, everyone else prances on their merry way, *(Indicating the audience in front of him...)* and no one's life is changed! Right? Right?!? Another play, over and done, and once again NOTHING REAL has happened!!

Well, this is just a stupid fucking play and maybe I don't want to shoot myself in the head! Maybe I want to go on like this forever, wallowing in in in self-pitying existential angst from production to production to production to production until the end of time! Maybe I want to go on *losing* and *failing* and *losing* and—

Oh, but wait! Then where's the catharsis? This is a "play" or what-ever, right, so we gotta have some kind of catharsis or you'll all want your fucking money back. So where's the catharsis? *(Calling off.)* Has anyone seen the catharsis? We didn't forget to bring it did we?!?! *(Dev comes on, and the others follow, either right away or even-tually...)* CAN A FELLA GET A LITTLE FUCKING CATHARSIS AROUND HERE OR NOT?!?!?

29. A Little Cap

DEV. Ummm... hey.
CON. Yeah?
DEV. You okay?
CON. Yeah.
DEV. You sure?
CON. No.
DEV. Oh?

CON. Yeah.

DEV. Okay. Okay...

CON. Ummm...

DEV. Yeah?

(This is by far the hardest thing for him—or anyone—to say in the entire play... This should be as "real" as possible, a true catharsis:)

CON. She... she's... ummm...

DEV. *(Gently.)* Breathe...

CON. ... she's never going to love me... is she? *(He cries... sobs, even...)*

DEV. No.

CON. *(Pushing on through...)* Not *ever*, right?

DEV. Right. Not ever...

CON. Oh, God...

DEV. I'm sorry, pal. I'm so, so sorry.

CON. Oh, God, I'm so fucked... *(To the audience. Small. Honest. Still wound tight, not backing relaxing, just retreating a moment...)* Sorry. Sorry. *(Con walks away. He paces or moves around the stage during all this.)*

DEV. *(To us.)* Okay. Shall we wrap it up here? Put a little cap on it? *(The other actors enter. This is not an improv—fake or real. They move to their places for the end...)* So, thank you all for coming here tonight. Here is what happens to each of the characters after the play ends. In case you're curious... I'll go first. For me, life just... goes, you know, *on*... We have some really nice moments, actually. Surprisingly lovely, even. Two of my kids do great, the other... less so. I live till I'm eighty-one. My last years, with my grandkids, are the best years.

MASH. We do fine. Good, I guess. Life life life, right? I die at sixty-one when a drunk driver hits me out of the fucking blue when I'm walking home from the farmer's market. Which, somehow, seems just about right.

SORN. I die in nine months. Uneventfully. Confused. Content.

EMMA. I do fine. I never get much happier—although I often have a wonderful time. Many people continue to just kind of hate me... though more quietly. I become an aging actress, with all that that brings. I die, exhausted, on my ninetieth birthday.

TRIGORIN. I would have to say... more of the same. Little dramas. Lots of writing. Fascinating. Mundane. "Superlative." A good life. I die quite happy.

76

Sorry.

NINA. *(Stepping forward.)* I go on. I just… go on.

CON. *(Pulling out a gun.)* I shoot myself.

(He puts the gun to his head. Leaves it there a beat. Poised to pull the trigger. Tense silence. Then he suddenly aims it at a light onstage, fires—the light explodes. The cast is freaked, screams, maybe.)

I fucking shoot myself! *(The stage is tense…)* Or not. *(Quick beat.)* Or…

(No one moves. They are bracing for a shot. Beat. Con turns to the audience.)

Stop the fucking play.

(Blackout.)

End of Play

PROPERTY LIST

Makeup
Curtain
Life Savers candy
Copy of Con's play
Note
Bloody bird-filled sack
Ukulele
Drinks
Bag of pecans
Blender, ingredients for berry smoothie
Implements and ingredients to make a cocktail
Implements and ingredients to make a peanut butter and jam
    sandwich, or an apple
Bass, or another ukulele
Party decorations
Birthday cake with lit candles

SOUND EFFECTS

Loud gunshots
Hum of the refrigerator

9780822232506